To Rolf

Endless Beginnings

The Learning of a Life Lesson

Arlette Noirclerc

iUniverse, Inc.
Bloomington

ENDLESS BEGINNINGS
THE LEARNING OF A LIFE LESSON

iUniverse books may be ordered through booksellers or by contacting:

iUniverse
1663 Liberty Drive1
Bloomington, IN 47403
www.iuniverse.com
1-800-Authors (1-800-288-4677)

Because of the dynamic nature of the Internet, any web addresses or links contained in this book may have changed since publication and may no longer be valid. The views expressed in this work are solely those of the author and do not necessarily reflect the views of the publisher, and the publisher hereby disclaims any responsibility for them.

Any people depicted in stock imagery provided by Thinkstock are models, and such images are being used for illustrative purposes only.

Certain stock imagery © Thinkstock.

ISBN: 978-1-4759-7692-2 (sc)
ISBN: 978-1-4759-7693-9 (hc)
ISBN: 978-1-4759-7694-6 (e)

Library of Congress Control Number: 2013902869

Printed in the United States of America

iUniverse rev. date: 3/29/2013

Dedication

I want to thank my family, friends and people who crossed my path in helping me understand the lessons I had to learn in life. Their interactions and my experiences made me the person I am today. Finally, I would like to acknowledge the Unitarian Universalist churches, which were the perfect homes for me, thanks to their understanding and recognition of the liberty and beliefs of all people. They made it possible for me to reconcile my old beliefs with the new ones I found along the way.

Table of Contents

Part Three

Part Four

Part Five

Prologue

I once read that a soul mate is the person who inflicts on you the worst pains because through those pains you learn the most and therefore receive the most.

We learn through hard times and great joys. The changes in my life were not by accident. I reached the conclusion that the obstacles thrown in my path by powerful forces caused me to explore a spiritual world I had not always believed in. The results of my search would eventually lead to the beliefs I hold today.

Some judged my life as unstable. But the ever-new beginnings were necessary to bring me to a place where I would know peace, tranquility and clarity. It took a war, a trip half-way around the world, two broken marriages, a violent attack, numerous affairs, major operations, several business ventures, many moves around the country, numerous workshops and meetings with great spiritual teachers and, above all, the love of my children to mold my heart and soul and achieve a healthy mental, physical and spiritual life.

I took many chances, often acted impulsively and sometimes too quickly, but as I learned through books and experiences, I always felt guided. My decisions were made when I got a feeling that some action was the best thing to do at the time. I hesitated rarely, knowing I was following what was laid out for me. Eventually I would understand that the hardships were lessons, the joys were gifts and that things happen for a reason.

This book was conceived in the spring of 2006, when I was wondering if my patience was being tested again or if there was something else being asked of me. I had been at a crossroad, contemplating a new life and this new dilemma struck a chord in my mind. Finding another beginning was what I had been doing all my life and I was good at it.

I had sold my last business, a fashionable shop in the heart of Sarasota, Florida and I knew it was time to make drastic changes that included selling my house and planning my retirement. Florida was in a downspin real-estate bubble and properties were slow to change hands. As long as my house was not sold, my life remained at a standstill.

Then, one morning the strongest feeling of what to do next came over me: The story of my life had to be told. I sensed that others would benefit from knowing about my experiences, which had shown me the way to a sense of peace. It would tell how the universe has laws that have to be learned and respected.

My story would recall the circumstances, people and events that had changed my life. It would tell about my search and the tribulations of a gypsy-like, dynamic life that forced me to look for people who would influence me and help me get to the place in life I cherish today. Joy and pain had brought me here and I always had powerful forces and people helping me along the way.

Born in France with too much, I was selfish and uncaring as a youth. My destiny placed me at birth in an environment too restrictive for me to learn the true principles of life. My mother had been brought up by very strict parents who never accepted her free spirit and individuality. She married a man who adored her but had little in common with her. My father always wanted to do the right thing, but he never understood his own children. He thought his role was to tell them what to think instead of helping them develop their own minds. They were loving parents but had a hard time bringing up their teenage children as Protestants in a predominantly Roman Catholic country and a harder time coping with the German occupation during World War II. The aftermath of the war added more problems.

Food was hard to find and people held resentments towards one another because of their political beliefs.

Too many ups and downs at home created an atmosphere I wanted to escape. Being the third one of the family, I was treated like a baby and nobody had any interest in what I had to say. I felt alone in a world that was scarred by the war and was just starting to set aside the memory of its atrocities. I dreamed of other shores and wanted to have fun and move away from it all.

The universe would eventually propel me into a life that would give me all the tools and experiences necessary to grow beyond my limited circumstances. I discovered that there are universal laws guiding us ever so gently and I had to learn them. After years of reading and sharing my thoughts with others, I eventually did learn these universal laws and I was able to read and accept the signs showing me the way. These signs became more obvious as I learned to pay more attention to what was going on around me.

So I hope my story will bring some clarity to the people I love the most, but also to others who might use it to make more sense of what appears to be complete chaos in their own life.

Part One

Chapter One

Learning to Walk Alone

Very early one April morning in 1935 in the city of Fontainebleau, seventy miles south of Paris, I came into the world. Shortly after I was born, my family moved to Versailles near the palace of Versailles and Paris, where my father began working in the headquarters of the company where he was employed.

My brother and sister, Dany and Roby, were very close in age, nearly twins, five and six years older than I. They did everything together and their private world was disrupted when their baby sister appeared. They never played with or had any interest in me and I never tried to understand why they left me alone. I was quite content and did not feel left out because I thought they were too old to play with me.

My isolation turned out to be a blessing as it forced me to look elsewhere for companionships. Later on, my love for people and the burning desire to express my feelings made me develop many friendships all over the world.

My ally was my father. He was a busy man, an engineer and general manager of a large business making electric cables. But when it came to me, he always had time and stopped what he was doing for a few minutes to listen to my stories. I still remember hiding under his huge desk while he smiled at my mother opening the door of his office to check if I had not intruded again. She had caught me many times in the sanctity of this room and had taken me away to let my father work undisturbed by my childish verbiage. He called me "Alouette" and was a god to me.

World War II was raging outside my world and food was rationed. But my father made sure we always had what we needed. Whenever he went to visit his company factory in Normandy he would visit some local farmers to get a ham, sausages or delicious jam to bring home.

While he was coming back from one of his food expeditions one day, his train did not stop in Versailles. Instead, it slowed down enough so that he could jump out. He had to throw his briefcase to the ground before making the jump himself. When he arrived home and opened his briefcase, to the family's dismay we had to throw away just about everything he was carrying. The glass container of the precious jam had shattered into small pieces, making it too dangerous to eat anything he so carefully transported back for us.

At the time, Versailles was in the occupied zone and we had stopped going to our seaside vacation home because it was in the free zone and you could not go from the occupied zone to the free zone without passes and approval from the authorities. Some people could not leave the occupied zone at all.

During these troubled times I learned what fear was. The German army was everywhere. You could not step out of the apartment building without seeing soldiers and officers everywhere. I was afraid of their shiny swords with silver ornaments and tassels The German language and its guttural sounds became part of my world.

As a five-year-old I heard grownups talking about what was going on around us, people who were arrested, the fear people were living under and the food shortage. I used to hide and listen to what they were saying and I grasped the meaning of the horrors that people who had been arrested experienced.

I learned early to avoid all these infamous warriors. I remember once walking along the avenue, looking down, completely lost in my own childish dreams, when accidentally I bumped into one of the dreaded enemy giants. I was so small and he was so tall.

At that moment, the ground disappeared under me. Was I going to be taken away from my mother? I feared that the stories I had heard were about to become my reality. All the nervousness, fear and anxiety surfaced in a split second. But I did not have time to dwell on this. The giant simply smiled at me and walked away.

Utterly confused, not understanding what had just happened, I asked my mother why I was not taken away. "You're just a little girl," said my mother, laughingly. But this answer was not good enough for me. I needed to understand why those giants could have good feelings sometimes and be so cruel at other times. This was the first time in my life I started questioning facts.

What was complicated for me to understand then would become clear much later in life, that people are very complex and can show good and bad intentions. I believe it was one of the first exercises given to me by the universe to sharpen my mind. Young children of five or six years of age often have spontaneous reasoning, which can be amazingly accurate before experiences, good or bad, teach them to copy their peers. In losing their innocence, they often lose their natural instincts and truthfulness.

One thing I remember about the German occupation was going to school with a tiny gas mask designed for young children. There were two small bottles and a gauze pad in the bag containing the gas mask. I was told by my mother how to use it. You first place a few drops from the number one bottle on the gauze pad and then add a few drops from the number two bottle. Place the pad inside the mask and then place the mask on your face, making sure you secure the nose clip on your nose. It was all very matter-of-fact. But we had been told that gas killed people, so it was scary to me as a five-year old.

The school where I attended kindergarten was in an old stone building about a mile away from home. Most of the time my mother walked me to school. When she could not, our long-time housekeeper, Maria, went with me and held my hand tightly, as if she was afraid I would run off. It seemed everyone was nervous at the time.

Kindergarten was fun because I made many friends there.

But I had a hard time with my teacher who was determined to force me to use my right hand to write. A slap of her pencil on my fingers reminded me often that being left-handed was totally inexcusable in those days.

That same year at Christmastime I experienced the first moment of pure and complete joy in my life. My sister, brother and I had been sleeping in the same room as there were only two heated bedrooms in the huge apartment. On Christmas morning, we were just waking up when my mother asked us to come and join her and my father in their bedroom to see all the presents Santa had brought us. The three of us eagerly jumped out of bed and went to their bedroom.

I unwrapped my first present as fast as I could and, when I saw it, I went into a state of what I can only describe today as ecstasy.

There it was, the doll I had admired in the toy shop we visited on many occasions was now in my arms. It was the most precious and beautiful thing I had ever seen. It looked like a real baby, the size of a three-month-old with soft arms and legs. What fascinated me were her eyes, which could open and close and had long eyelashes. The doll was an expensive present and a little extravagant for a little girl, but my mother understood what it meant to me and bought it just in time for Christmas.

I had few friends at that age, so I played with my doll all the time.

When I was twenty four and moved to the U.S., I was very upset to find out that my parents had disposed of her. Still, the doll and the wonderful times I experienced with her stayed engraved in my memory as the happiest of those difficult times.

This gift of joy from my mother at such an early age helped me later in life to understand how deep children's feelings are and how important it is to acknowledge them. Discipline is a must, but a little pampering goes a long way. The best proof of this is that seventy years later, I still remember a doll given to me by a loving mother.

When I was seven years old I wanted a bird. My mother explained to me that birds should be free to fly in the sky and that it would be sad to have one in the house. She did not convince me, so I looked at pictures to learn more about birds. I imagined my bird different from other birds, as he would enjoy his cage and be happy to be in my care. I would talk to him when I woke up and say good night in the evening. From a very early age I knew what I wanted and rarely changed my mind, which made it difficult for my parents to get their way.

Within a few months after speaking with my mother about getting a bird, I put my allowance aside and, with the help of my older sister, bought some bird seed. My mother was convinced that I would eventually renounce my bird fantasy, so she let me keep my bird seed in my room, provided that it was stored in an aluminum box to keep bugs away. But I kept putting my allowance aside.

After one year, I had enough to buy a bird cage. By this time my mother was ready to give up the battle of wills. "You have shown me how much you want a bird and you have been patient and stubborn enough to go on with your dream," she said, "so I will help you. You buy the cage and I will buy you the bird."

My bird was beautiful. It was like a canary with gorgeous yellow coloring. I called him Kiki and he had the cleanest cage any bird ever had. He became my confidante and companion and was the one friend I could sing with and share all my stories about how difficult it was to be the third one in the family and to be ignored most of the time.

I even trained him to fly out and back in the cage, to the exasperation of our housekeeper who kept finding droppings all over the apartment. For the first time in my life I was in love and everybody agreed that Kiki had been a great addition to the family, as everybody was fond of him.

But my first love story would not last. I used to place Kiki's cage on the living room balcony so he could get some fresh air. But one sad day, I placed the cage on the balcony without properly securing the door. Then, to my horror, right before my eyes the cage door opened and Kiki flew out.

The apartment was on the third floor of the building and at first it looked like Kiki was flying down. But as soon as he reached the ground, my mother and I realized he could not fly a long distance. He had been born in a cage and only flew very short distances inside the apartment. We rushed downstairs and followed him. We thought we could catch him, but each time we got close, he would fly a little further out of our reach. Eventually, we had to return home. I longed for him to return on his own, but he never came back. My mother promised to buy me another bird, but I refused. I only wanted my Kiki back.

Time passed and, when my heart healed, I was ready for another bird. But I asked for a different kind, as I did not want to be reminded of Kiki. So my mother bought me an exotic red beak Mandarin. She had heard that Mandarins were magical and revered in the Orient, so I thought this was a good sign. Nonetheless, this time I did not let my bird out of the cage and I always made sure the door was securely fastened when I put the cage on the balcony. I was quite satisfied with my new friend.

One sunny day, I heard a lot of noise, chirping and singing loudly. Intrigued by what was happening, I rushed to the balcony and could not believe my eyes. Another red beak Mandarin was on top of the cage singing along with my own bird. Where did this stranger come from? Versailles was not a place where one expects to find exotic birds. The only explanation I could come up with was that he escaped from another cage and heard my bird calling him, unless something else attracted him from very far away. Whatever the reason, he came back day after day. I thought the right thing to do would be to catch him and put him in the cage as he would be safer in the cage. But my mother convinced me otherwise. "He has been able to get around quite safely on his own up till now, so there is no reason for us to put him in a cage. Besides," she added, "his owner might be looking for him." After a week he disappeared and we never saw him again.

I realized that nature is full of mysteries. The appearance and disappearance of this exotic bird in the middle of a big city, with no trees close by, was one mystery I would question for quite some time. I have lived a long life and heard of, or witnessed, experiments that seemed to be beyond our power. But to this day, I still wonder about the miracle of that episode. Can a single bird create such vibrations that it can attract another bird of the same breed from faraway? It seems to me that this is when nature and the universe work together to create perfect harmony.

Chapter Two

Building My Imagination

A few years later, my mother gave me a tiny room to use as a playroom. It became mine, my very own domain. In that room I built a tent made out of blankets, sheets and rugs that I had gathered from all over the apartment, creating an exotic place which helped me escape to a world of make-believe. It was at this early age of ten that I developed a vivid imagination, which was going to be a leading force in my finding solutions to challenges throughout my life. In that tent I learned to be by myself, to play, think and dream.

My dreams were big. Living near the palace of Versailles, every day I was taken to the palace's huge gardens to run and play with other children. The shadows of the ancient place, the infinite staircases, the statues looking down at me, the oversized lanes that went on forever and the murmur of the flowing fountains, added some flamboyant scenes to my girlish imagination. It was in my tent, back in my playroom, that I took my first travels to unknown lands, worlds far away from home.

These memories shaped my view, so much so that today, I have a hard time seeing children needing more and more manufactured toys and young parents having the notion that they must entertain their children at all times. I know that times have changed and that today's education is different than from the time I raised my own children. I am not judging new parents or the progress in education, but only wondering, how this new generation, used to get immediate gratification will cope if their world ever collapses.

Alone in my tent, I learned to create my own enjoyment, to read books and to create an environment of make-believe. These activities would later contribute to my never-ending search for ways to make things in my life better.

The only problem I had at the time was that Roby did not seem to appreciate having a younger sister who, he apparently thought, was always in his way. I often had the feeling he thought of me as the enemy and was glad for the fact that he was five years older and stronger.

He became part of the lessons I had to learn about the universe. But as a child I could not understand why he acted with hostility towards me and I often hoped for better days.

Eventually he got tired of bullying me and, by the time I was fifteen, my brother and I became such good friends that I became his confidante and he became my mentor. I would learn a lot from him when it came to communicating with the other sex and understanding the differences between men and women.

But Roby continued to shape my life. Through the bad years and the good ones, I learned many lessons from him. Our relationship made me stronger, forced me to fend for myself and helped me think on my feet.

———

It was in 1944, when we were living in Versailles, that my childhood world was forever changed, when my father announced that we had to move away from the city. As the liberation by the allies appeared to be near, he decided we should be as far away as possible from cities like Versailles and Paris. He wanted us to be in a small village where it would be much quieter and safer for us.

Unfortunately, he unwittingly chose a location that would eventually become a central battleground. The village he chose was in the heart of Normandy. It was there that my destiny would bring me, at the age of nine, face-to-face with war and, more significantly, with my very first American friends.

We moved into a hotel in the center of Alençon, which would be our home base until we could find a permanent place to stay. My days there were spent reading and learning how to knit. My mother tried hard to occupy our time while my father was out all day looking for a new home for us.

Soon after we arrived, I became very sick and a doctor was called in. He told my mother he thought it was diphtheria and warned us not to go anywhere before confirming what it was. It would take twenty-four hours for the throat culture to develop. The next day, when my parents stopped by the hospital to get the results, a nurse informed them that I did not have diphtheria, but that we had to wait for an official written report from the doctor. The town, the hospital and the doctor were controlled by the Germans and they were very afraid of illness.

When we received the doctor's report, we were dismayed to read that I was indeed diagnosed with diphtheria and that we had to leave the hotel within one day or could be arrested. We did not know for sure what I had, but we believed the nurse had accurately told us I did not have diphtheria and that the German authorities ordered the final report to be altered. This ensured that I would not go to the hospital, as a German declaration forbade any contagious disease to be treated in the hospital while there were German soldiers there.

We did not know what to do. Before leaving the hotel, I had to be given a serum in the stomach with an enormous needle. It took three people, my mother, the nurse and the doctor, to hold me down during the injection. My screams must have been heard all over the floor and they tried to keep me quiet, so as not to attract unwanted attention from our enemies. The German army never took any chances when it came to contagious illnesses.

Luckily, my father found an Australian family living in a huge house willing to take us in the next day. Their large manor could easily accommodate two families without being crowded as there were two wings to the mansion.

It was decided that my mother and I would move in for two

weeks, during which we would not come out of our room until the danger had cleared. Then the rest of the family would join us and we would stay with the Australians in their home until the occupation was over, however long it would take.

I recuperated so quickly that we all soon knew I never had the terrifying disease in the first place. But my false diagnosis turned out to be a blessing in disguise. Our Australian host had made a huge sign in German saying: "Achtung. Do not enter this domain, Diphtheria." The result was that, during our entire stay, we never saw a motorcycle or a German car driving down the road leading to the manor.

Once we were all reunited and got settled in our new home, we discovered the wonders of this enchanting place. Next to the house there was a farm that was part of the estate and it soon became my favorite place. We became friends with the other children at the estate and had lots of fun experiencing for the first time what life was like in a country farm. It also meant better food and more of it. We felt completely free.

The only restriction placed on us was the duty to rush home or take shelter at the sound of the whistle that my fifteen-year-old sister kept around her neck at all times. She used it quite often when she perceived danger of any kind, including when P 38 lightning planes flew on the horizon. We knew they were flown by Americans dropping bombs on German targets and we always welcomed them regardless of the damage they created. The price paid was small compared to the German occupation and we knew it was necessary to finally be free.

With D-Day approaching, the bombings became more intense, as the planes targeted the town of Alençon and its manufacturing plants only a few miles away. My father's plant was among them and, as general manager, he had no choice but to work surrounded by German officers.

What a nightmare it must have been for him to work there, while armed Germans made sure the factory ran smoothly. Apart from all the questionable breakdowns and the known *maquisarts* (French resistance fighters) working in the factory, I wonder how many times a day he asked himself what to do.

Refuse orders? Run away? And what if he was shot? He knew his family, wife and children would be in danger.

I believe you don't have much of a choice when the reality of torture and death threaten the people you love the most. So, he kept on working there, everyday going to Alençon on his bicycle, since civilian use of motor vehicles was no longer permitted. I think that at night, when he was home with his family, he was praying the planes would hit their target.

One night, he did not come home. He was injured on his way to work when a bomb exploded nearby and he ended up in the hospital. He sustained shrapnel injuries and was found in a ditch covered with dirt. Luckily, he recovered. Waiting for him that night had been hard for us at home. We did not know whether he would come back or not, or whether he had been arrested, which my mother also feared.

Today, military uniforms still make me uncomfortable. Even seeing customs officials at the airport and police officers in the city sometimes gives me an uneasy feeling. I have had to work especially hard to remove such fear from my life.

It seems my brother and sister did not develop the same scars. Being older, they handled their emotions better and were able to forget aspects of the war that haunted me and their recollection of certain details of the war was quite different from mine.

Chapter Three

The Liberation

I t had been several hours since the rumbling had begun. We knew it was from tanks because our parents told us. At first it felt like the roaring of machines and as it continued, the sensation of the earth moving under our feet became more pronounced. The clanking of steel tank treads joined the noise of the engines. The wheels that guided the long metal ribbons kept turning. It all brought chills to my body. It was still 1944 and I was nine years old; my brother was thirteen and my sister fifteen. We knew the war was raging on the beaches, but we had not yet seen any sign of soldiers other than the Germans. Now we heard the first tanks to show up in our village.

Unable to stand our curiosity and despite our parents' protests, we rushed out of the house towards the main road to see them. At first, we were surprised, because the soldiers in the tanks were French and yet they did not stop to talk. Instead, they shouted at us to go back inside, back to our parents. Roby and I did what we were told, but my older sister stayed behind. We had hardly reached the gate of the house when we heard shooting. But this was no battle. It was a single sniper shooting at my sister. The soldiers in the tanks had been trying to protect us. The area was full of German soldiers fighting for their lives and it was not safe for us to be running around. My sister immediately realized the danger she was in as the bullets flew by, barely missing her. She came flying home, losing her shoes in the process. Once inside the safe haven of the house, she collapsed and started to cry. My mother let her cry and then she turned to the three of us and said, "This should be a good lesson." She added, "In these uncertain days, we should be more careful when going out."

War, fear and danger make people more resilient. My mother knew this and it was no time for pity. We knew she loved us. She was devastated that her children had to live through all this. During the Normandy invasion, my parents never showed signs of weakness. They were our rocks and, like most children, we knew they had the answers and knew what to do.

Thinking back, I wonder why my mother did not simply forbid us to go outside. I think she forced herself to believe we could lead a normal life, even though these were not normal times. I am sure she did the best she could under the circumstances.

A few days later, my mother and I went to a nearby farm to get some fresh eggs. We saw a tank on the side of the road, with men leisurely lounging around it and smoking cigarettes. It was a British tank and my mother decided she wanted to practice her English, so we stopped by for a while and talked to the men. We had been there for less than ten minutes when we were shot at by another tank. In a split second, the soldiers pushed us behind the tank, jumped inside and started to fire back. Fortunately for us the German tank quit firing. I don't know why they fired only once or why they stopped. But we had been spared once more, protected and saved from our own carelessness.

We would have forgotten about that incident if it were not for the fact that, after we were liberated by the Americans, we found that same German tank in a nearby field, burned to the ground, the charred debris of what was once the glory of Hitler's glorious Panzers.

At long last they came. Our liberators and saviors stormed the beaches of Normandy. As many fell to their deaths, others kept on coming. They were getting closer every day.

We were sleeping with our clothes on when, one night in

June 1944, the noise of the bombing became deafening. My father opened the wooden shutters and we saw that under the darkness outside, the sky was illuminated, bright orange as in the middle of a stormy day when the lightning strikes. "Come children, it's time to go," he said in a voice as calm as he could make it. "It's time to go to the shelter."

The house we lived in with our Australian friends was too much of a target for the bombers. We and our house-mates had two shelters built close to the edge of a field for times such as this. The two shacks were made of wood with aluminum roofs and had been built primarily to protect us from the rain or sun, but also to store a few necessary items like blankets and pillows.

That night, our two families ran for their lives through the Normandy fields. It was difficult for us, especially the five barefoot children, to ignore the thundering noise, the explosions and the smell of fumes and smoke all around.

Once in the shelter, my father told us, "Lie flat on the grass and keep your heads down." I was too scared to look and was glad to oblige.

I believe I must have slept out of sheer exhaustion because I don't remember anything else. When I woke up the following morning and raised my head, I found our new American friends surrounding us. They were all over the field. They had arrived during the night, but with the noise of the bombing we never knew that about three hundred men had walked into our field and our lives.

None of us will ever forget the feeling of excitement, gratitude and happiness we all felt at that moment. In her broken English my mother asked one of the soldiers only a few feet away: "Were you scared last night?"

"Oh yes, for sure we were. What about you?"

With this short dialogue I had my first glimpse of a real American hero. The Australians were already making new friends as their language allowed them to understand everything the Americans were saying.

My parents were discussing what to do next when I decided

to get my shoes. I started back to the house but stopped after a few feet as the spikes of cut wheat and small stones on the ground made me cry for help. Somebody else had to get them for me. It was at that moment that I realized how scared I must have been the night before as I never even felt any pain in my feet while running towards the shelter.

In later years I learned more about the phenomenon of mind over matter and used different techniques to suppress pain. I remembered that on that very night without knowing it, I had my first experience of having controlled pain by being totally absorbed by what was happening and concentrating on running.

My brother found himself surrounded by three soldiers after my mother told them that he had seen a parachute land the night before in a nearby area. They asked Roby to go with them to look for what they thought would be a dead body or a live comrade. To everybody's delight it turned out to be a parachute used to carry a very large flare, not the dreaded dead body. For his keen observation and courage, Roby was given the chute, which he still has, as a reminder of that day.

Shortly after that, one of the officers asked if they could use part of the house as a makeshift hospital before transporting their wounded soldiers to a more permanent place. Of course, everybody agreed to their request, so happy to be able to do something for the troops. Then, my mother asked, "What can we do to help, in addition to sharing the house?"

The answer was short and easy. "Could you cook us a meal with French fries the way you cook them in France?"

Laughingly, my mother replied, "I can cook whatever you want as long as you provide the ingredients missing from our depleted kitchens."

The young officer motioned my brother to his jeep and explained, "We're going straight to our central headquarters and will be back shortly." About an hour later they came back carrying a twenty-pound bag of potatoes, meat and a huge box full of assorted cheeses, to the delight of everybody.

They showered us with candies, chewing gum, K packages

(which had their daily food rations) and their loving attention. The only unhappy one was my sister who, looking older than her fifteen years, got silk stockings instead of chocolates.

It is in that Normandy village, in a time of sorrow and joy that all of us experienced true communication with people we had never known before. These men came a long way to fight a common enemy and they survived a battle that cost many, many lives. They were exhausted. Yet they took the time to play with us children, talk to the adults and relate their war experiences to us. For this moment in their lives, they looked truly happy to share their experiences and feelings with us. We could not always understand what they were saying, but nobody needed words to express the gratitude and connection we all felt.

The arrival of the Americans did not immediately stop the fighting around us, as they had to make sure no Germans were left behind. So our friends had to go from field to field and house to house to capture the last ones. As much as we lacked sympathy for the occupiers, I have to acknowledge the courage of the Germans who remained in and around the village. They fought to their last breath knowing quite well it was the end for them. The ones who surrendered were rounded up in the courtyard of the farm, ordered to place their hands over their heads and were taken away by truck.

Today I marvel at the resilience of children and their ability to erase or forget bad memories. One wonders sometimes how children who have witnessed atrocities can function normally after being exposed to so much.

Our American friends were prepared to leave and were saying good-bye. One of the soldiers insisted on giving my brother his motorcycle, that is, if my parents would let him. Of course, my parents refused. "We appreciate your offer, but it is out of the question. He is only thirteen," they said. Roby hardly talked to them for days, as he had a hard time accepting his disappointment.

It was painful to see the American soldiers pull out of our village after sharing so much together. But life soon went back to normal in the absence of the bombings and the fear.

After the first troops left, others came: The English, the French and more Americans. But they were not like our first heroes. They were polite but did not have the same perspective. After all, they did not suffer on the beaches. They did not have the profound gratitude and excitement of being alive, which the others had shared with us.

It is such a different experience to hear about a war while being safe and far away. But having been there, one never forgets the fear and anxiety that war imposes on the psyche. As I recall my first encounter with war, I ache to think of the courage needed by our men and women in uniform to be able to perform their heroic duties.

I wonder, could it be the intense feeling of joy and admiration I felt at first seeing these brave Americans in Normandy that later influenced my decision to go to the United States? I believe in some ways, it was.

The war and the liberation had an impact on me that I did not quite understand at first, but later on I faced the fact that the fear instilled in me during these dramatic years would leave residues. My trauma came from hearing too much bombs exploding around us, too much fear of being taken by the Germans, too much witnessing of people being dragged away and I was twenty-six when I finally stopped having recurring nightmares of German soldiers chasing me. I kept running and running until I woke up, sometimes screaming. All my life I had all sorts of anxiety attacks that I had to learn to control with meditation and, at times, with medication. Even when I have had nothing to fear, I have felt symptoms in my body similar to the ones I had when the war was on.

In the nineteen fifties, tensions were rising between France and Algeria, which was eager to gain independence from the French government. When Roby was in his early twenties, he was drafted as a paratrooper to serve there. This was a terrible time for my family.

Roby was part of a special detachment, the eleventh choc

battalion, which took orders directly from the war ministry. At all times, they needed to be prepared to drop into the most rebellious areas on a minute's notice. His role as a lieutenant was to maintain the peace and look for some of the most sought-after and dangerous *fellagas*, people taking part in the rebellion against the French government. Because he was part of a secret unit, he could not give us an address to reach him so we could not communicate with him except when he called home. Newspapers reported the names of his fallen comrades-in-arms and we lived day-to-day waiting to hear whether he was alive or dead.

When he finally came home, he was very different. He was quieter and more cynical about life and death. He refused to give details about the war. He just said that wars brought out the worst in people, especially those whose morality was questionable. He added that he felt sorry for many of his men, especially the wounded, whom he could not get out of his mind. He kept in touch with quite a few of them and visited them throughout his life.

The Algerian war would destroy many people and pit Frenchman against Frenchman. It took years to heal the people involved and the strength of President Charles de Gaulle to grant Algeria independence and restore peace to France which struggled with internal turmoil.

Chapter Four

Teenage Years

The war had taken a high toll on the population. People had to rebuild their houses, forgive their neighbors' denunciation to the Gestapo, forget the horrors of torture and accept the loss of many cherished family members and friends. I was fortunate in that my immediate family had been spared and most of my cousins and uncles also survived.

When I entered my teens I wanted to forget the war and started to be more interested in making friends and lots of them. Whether boys or girls, it made no difference to me; they were my friends.

But when I reached the age of fifteen I became quite aware of the difference and started to enjoy the attention I received from the opposite sex. It would not be long before my parents started to worry and imposed on me a very strict schedule to keep me busy. In my parents' eyes, I should wait till eighteen before going out with any young man, regardless of how well-behaved he was. They wanted to make sure the fun I was having would stay innocent for as long as they could have their say.

At sixteen, I convinced my parents to allow me to enter a well-known art school in Paris known as "Les Arts Decoratifs" to learn design, interior decorating and graphic arts. I did not know at first what my lifelong career would be, but I knew that art would be a major factor in my life and would take me later on from interior decorating to fashion designing.

I thrived in my new school environment, but the schedule was grueling. Having returned with my family to live in Versailles, I had to take a train every day at 6 o'clock to be on time for my 8 o'clock class. So my parents agreed to rent a room in Paris for me in a youth hostel for young ladies. I was happy to be on my own, especially because the pension was next door to an art cinema showing Hitchcock movies around the clock.

At first, I took some general design courses and discovered that I could use both my hands to design. Having been forced to write with my right hand in elementary school, I was relieved that my teacher encouraged me to use my left hand as much as possible. He believed strongly that it would alleviate some of the problems I was having, such as not being able to discern right from left and inverting letters of the alphabet when I was writing. He was right. After four years of art school I was cured.

In the beginning, the charcoal courses were my favorites. We never knew in advance whether the live models would be males or females and, when it was a male model, there was a lot of giggling. But as time went by, it became just another routine course.

I finally graduated with a degree in interior design. But it would be decades before I went into this field, as life was going to throw me first into the world of fashion.

———◦◦◦———

My family and I began to return to our cherished island of Oléron a year after the war was over. Known for its beautiful beaches in the Atlantic Ocean, Oléron is a popular destination for summer vacationers. Today, it is connected to the mainland by a bridge, but when I was a child we had to get there by boat. Oléron was paradise to me. We knew everybody there.

My grandfather first took his seven children there in 1906 and made friends with two other families that came in the summer to that small village of La Remigeasse. The two hundred people who lived there all year were mostly farmers who grew grapes to make wine to supplement their incomes. In the summer, the village doubled in size. As the families grew and brought friends, the village expanded. Too many people came and loved the place. They had their own homes built and our cherished little village became larger and larger, until the edge of the village touched the edge of the neighboring one.

As soon as we arrived there every summer, we would visit the local farmers to say hello and check on how they had fared the previous winter. They called us "les vacanciers," or vacationers and always had a special heart-warming drink, a local wine called Pineau, which is still one of my favorite aperitifs. The farmers and my parents often reminisced about my grandmother who had organized many plays and lovely evenings for the people in the village in the beginning of the 1900's, when my father was still a little boy.

Shortly after the war my father decided to have our own vacation house built there. We had been renting the same house for many years, but it did not make sense to keep on renting. Some friends of ours offered my father a part of their land. The property was perfect. It was prime land right off the dunes and only a short walk separated us from the most beautiful beach. We were lucky that our friends were willing to part with such a unique plot of land so we could build our dream house. At that time, the beach was deserted and only a privileged few would meet there to swim, talk and enjoy each other's company.

The four-bedroom house was simple, all on one floor, but we loved the brightness, the Mediterranean roof and the tile floors. It was surrounded by ornamental olive trees and pines. It was indeed a special place I remember as one of the best we ever lived in.

Those three summer months in Oléron were a time of relaxation and also a time of learning. This is where we developed our social skills and as young adults had our first dating experiences, most of the time without our parents knowing about them. It was there, at the age of sixteen that I had my first proposal of marriage. It made my mother very upset. Since I was the third one, she always saw me as the baby of the family. In a sense, she probably had not seen me grow up and thought I was still a young girl. I was not interested in the offer, but it made me realize I was popular with the opposite sex. It may be that this proposal was the beginning of a life-search for the right partner, which gave me joy and excitement but would demand a lot of adjustments, pain and learning.

—⟡—

It was in that little village that I met my first love. I was eighteen and Marc was much older. With a twelve-year difference in age, I should have known our relationship would not last. But I was young and in love for the first time.

He appeared in mid-summer, coming back from the United States where he had spent a couple of years. He fascinated me with his tales of the new world and was very enthusiastic recalling his life and experiences from New York to California. He was handsome, fun, interesting and different from any man I had known until that time. The attraction I felt was new to me and I could not wait to see him when he came to the beach for his daily swim.

We spent more and more time together and when he first kissed me while we were looking at the stars one night on the beach I thought I was transported to heaven. The relationship was innocent, but I fell hard for him. Neither of us expressed our emotions and I wondered if he ever felt love for me.

When the summer was over I wanted to stay with him, but my father interrupted the relationship very abruptly by ordering me back to Versailles. Having been an officer in the army during the war, my father knew how to confront my rebellious soul and I could never go against his will. I left Marc with a heavy heart and returned home, resenting my parents and blaming them for hurting me so badly. After my father's interference I never heard from Marc again and I found out shortly afterwards that he went back to the States.

It has been said you never forget your first love and I believe this is true. After all this time I can still feel those strong emotions and remember clearly that it took a whole year to stop crying myself to sleep. But my father had been right that the relationship was not good for me. I found out later that Marc was already involved with someone else in the United States.

It was a hard lesson to learn, but it made me mature in a way nothing else could have. I did not know this when it happened, but today I can see that it was my first true heartbreak and I did receive benefits from it. Part of the lesson was to accept the universe guiding me on a different path and forcing me to accept the end of a dream. It would make me stronger to face the future. The experience contributed greatly to my desire to go to the United States, which would turn out to change my entire life. The seed was planted in my mind, leaving me curious about this far-away land. I did not know what I was looking for, but I felt the key to my future was there. Adding to the liberation by the Americans, my experience with Marc would create a strong bond with the United States and eventually lead me to this country, which would soon become my home.

Chapter Five

The House of Dior

I t would take five years to fulfill my dream. My determination to live in the States was so strong that I believe the universe answered my wishes and in the most wonderful way. It guided me through a maze of choices leading me eventually to the outcome I wanted.

During the five years I lived at the pension in Paris, I finished art school. After that I went to England to attend a finishing school for foreigners to learn English. As luck would have it, the woman I was staying with was a personal friend of the director of Christian Dior in London.

Louise approached me one day and asked, "Would you be interested in working for about two weeks for my friend, who you know is the the number one person of the House of Dior." She added that it would be a well-paid position and that everything would be explained to me later.

The timing was perfect as I was just finishing my English courses and could take this short-term position without interfering with my studies or discussing it with my parents. "Oui, bien sur," I replied, eagerly. She made an appointment for the following day.

I was only twenty one and felt very intimidated when I walked into the plush office of the House of Dior. But I was quickly put at ease when a friendly voice said, "I am so delighted that you could come." Louise's friend started the interview by telling me that a French woman from the Paris office had been booked to give interviews and promote Dior accessories in England. "However," he went on, "she was suddenly fired a few days ago and there is not enough time to cancel her appearances." He was desperate to find a replacement and seemed eager for me to take her place. As he was explaining their difficult position, I started to appreciate how lucky I was.

He needed a mature representative who fit the Dior look. I appeared older than my twenty-one years of age, I was very slim and I wore my hair in the typical French twist that many models were flaunting at the time. It became clear that he knew I could fit the part. The glamour and money he offered for just a couple weeks of my time could not be refused.

For the next two weeks after my acceptance, I was molded by the House of Dior's well-oiled machine.

The intensive training included mornings, afternoons and evenings of hard work. There was much I had to absorb and memorize and details I had to know, from the manufacturing and marketing of certain products to what made the House of Dior so special. And I learned about the influence of the Boussac family, which financed the organization while making their fortune raising champion horses and winning races at Longchamp in the Bois de Boulogne. A team of one man and a woman prepared me to answer all kinds of questions about fashion, turned me into a real professional and threw me into a brand new life. In what seemed like an instant, I found myself absorbed in the amazing Dior machinery.

When my boss put me on the train from London to my first destination, Liverpool, he said to me, "If you don't know something, answer the best you can. But say something." This left me in a state of shock as I began to realize for the first time what I had accepted to do.

When I arrived in Liverpool, I was told I had to meet the press. No one had told me about this and I am sure the omission was done on purpose because I might not have been so eager to go if I knew what to expect. But I managed the best I could, feeling terrified inside as each reporter asked me a question. But after awhile I felt more confident. The questions seemed mostly about how it felt to work for Christian Dior, so I had more confidence as I went on to my other destinations.

After the newspaper interviews and meetings with managers of department stores, I started to lose some shyness that had plagued me since childhood. My photo even ended up in the local newspapers and I felt flattered that I made the news. The whole experience was fun and exciting.

When I returned to London I was told the trip was a great success and I had made a favorable impression on the executives at the home office in Paris. Not only did they want me to go on traveling for them, but Monsieur Rouet, the General Manager of the House of Dior, asked to meet me personally to discuss further employment.

The meeting took place in London with a few of the Dior executives. Monsieur Rouet said, "We need someone to travel all over the world to promote Dior products as one of our ambassadors." To my delight, he added, "You might have to go to South America or the United States."

Mr. Rouet asked if I could be ready upon short notice. When I answered yes, he told me I would first have to be trained in Paris and start as soon as possible.

After the meeting I was totally overwhelmed with emotion. It looked like my dream of going to the United States was becoming a reality. Looking back, I realized that it was more than just luck that guided my steps. It was a turn in the road directing my life towards my destiny.

My parents were not overjoyed to hear of my prospects and they had a hard time accepting that their youngest daughter was being thrown into the world of fashion. They believed that the luxury and glamour of the House of Dior would lead to a superficial life, not exactly what they envisioned for their daughter. But my mind was made up.

———⊷∞⊷———

My first day was not what anyone could have expected. Christian

Dior had died very suddenly and the entire firm was closed for business. I joined the others and attended the funeral.

The designer was immediately replaced by his assistant, Yves Saint Laurent, who, in a short time, would also become a fashion design guru. Yves Saint Laurent was able to plunge into a career that would bring him to the pinnacle of success.

The House of Dior had been built on the concept known as *haute couture* and it would survive long after its founder's death.

The original location was 30 Avenue Montaigne, but over the years several *hotels particuliers* belonging to neighboring owners were added. This created a very large compound with enough room for all the offices and ateliers where the garments were created.

The House of Dior in Paris is like a magnificent palace. Luxury is all around. From the sumptuous decors to the merchandise, colors, shapes, designs, scent and even the salespeople, everything is geared to please a difficult clientele representing the two percent wealthiest people in the world.

My lucky star must have been guiding me when I was given the incredible opportunity to be trained by the best in the world of *haute couture*. The outcome of my training at the House of Dior would give me a sense of fashion, quality and experience as well as the ability to work with the very powerful.

The excitement of learning in this never-sleeping environment shaped my life in some good and some bad ways. Unfortunately, I became accustomed to observing only what was superficially pleasing to my eyes. It took me years to stop being blinded by what shines brightly and fails to reflect one's inner nature. Nonetheless, my ability to see and know what was pleasing to the eye did benefit me later in my career.

One of the valuable lessons I learned was that a sense of style is not overdone. It is elegant and eternally stylish with a "je ne sais quoi" that makes it unique. It can be found in houses, in the countryside, in fashion and in people. The ones who have it cannot lose it and the ones who don't have it do not even know it. Some people have a natural ability to know how to choose clothes, or anything for that matter, without relying on a designer name or label. Over the years, in my long career in fashion, I met people, slim and heavy alike, who paid little for their clothes but knew how to choose what was right for them and they looked great in their selections. Others, who paid a lot for designer clothes, never looked right; too often, they were relying on inexperienced or hungry salespeople willing to take advantage of them.

I am forever grateful that my Dior training gave me confidence in my ability to know instinctively what is everlasting and how to ignore faddish trends. It would become the reason for my success in later years, when I plunged into fashion design and opened my own retail shops. It also gave me an edge over my competition and helped me survive when others failed.

My training program in Paris expanded on what I had learned in London about the great House of Dior and how garments were created. This included everything from the designing table to the final execution of the petite mains, the women finishing all the details of a specific piece by hand.

The program was going well, but my impatience to travel was growing. I was born for action and did not like waiting. So I was relieved when the order for my first assignment finally came. I would spend six months in the United States.

As an ambassador of the House of Dior, I was given a Dior wardrobe and, at the age of twenty-two, was thrilled to wear beautiful clothes that most people could not even dream of owning. The rule was that I had to return them after my trip or pay the equivalent of one cent on the dollar. In a business employing so many women who would have been envious of my wardrobe, it was necessary for me to be able to say I paid for the clothes.

Like me, France at the time was looking at the United States for inspiration. American movies were shown all over and they stirred my imagination. Cary Grant and Gregory Peck were the most handsome men on the big screen and I started to believe that all American men were just as handsome. American movies ended like fairy tales, both on and off-screen. After all, this was when Grace Kelly married her real-life prince, in April 1956. Her last movie, *High Society*, with its glamorous stars, was a huge success in France and I could not wait to discover the country where it was filmed.

And so it was that I found myself one day with huge suitcases on a propeller plane that would take fourteen hours to take me to my dream destination. TWA had berths for people to sleep comfortably and gave special treatment to the few of us privileged enough to fly first class. Under these circumstances, the trip did not seem long at all.

After clearing customs in New York, it was immediately evident that I had arrived in a different land when my American boss, who was waiting for me, said, "Call me Dick." Considering the formal background I had been used to in the House of Dior, this greeting was just as foreign to me as the language he spoke.

With mother, brother and sister. I am the baby.

1937. I was two years old.

Sweet Sixteen. Oléron, France

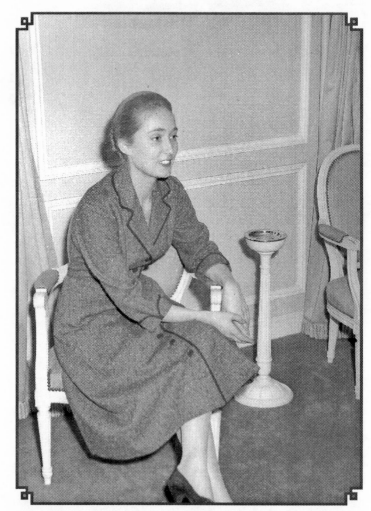

House of Dior

My parents

*My brother Roby was a French
champion hot-air balloon pilot.*

Part Two

Chapter Six

Land of Vision and Dreams

A limousine was waiting to take us to Manhattan, where I would be spending the night. Richard, or so I called my new boss, as I could not reconcile myself to addressing him in such a familiar way as Dick, wanted to make sure I was well-rested before going on to Chicago, so he made a reservation at the Gorham Hotel, one block from Central Park. It was a cold February and snow was falling ever so lightly, forming a white blanket over the trees and buildings. I declined to have dinner out because I was exhausted and asked instead to have a light supper brought to my room. We said goodnight and I went up to my room on the thirty-second floor. This was my first skyscraper experience. I was thrilled by the sensation of going up so fast in the elevator and the strange buzzing in my ears. I finished my dinner, went to bed and fell asleep. I was awakened the next morning by the phone ringing.

Richard was on the phone. "We are in the middle of a blizzard and all the planes have been grounded. I'll have to find another way to get out of the city." I looked out the window and there was snow everywhere. "Get ready to leave and I'll call you when I have our travel plans."

An hour later he called back. "I couldn't get a train reservation because all the trains are packed with stranded travelers. What we need to do is go to Grand Central Station anyhow. We'll have a better chance to fight our way through the lines there."

He was right. After bribing the right people, we were given two tickets with sleeping berths. This was much to my relief, as I was starting to get worried. I had never seen such a huge amount of snow and thought we would have to remain in New York for a long time. I was not aware of the great snow removal power that the Americans possessed. As I found out, it was just another blizzard New York went through, sort of a routine winter hazard.

Chicago would become my base for two weeks out of every month, during which I would travel throughout the Midwest representing the House of Dior. Richard would coordinate my activities from his office in New York. As soon as we arrived, he helped me find an apartment. Then he introduced me to the manager of Marshall Fields, who introduced me to the man who would be by Chicago contact.

During my first encounter with Marshall Fields, I was surprised that I was fingerprinted and given a Social Security number, since my income came from and stayed in France. I just assumed it was the American way of doing business. So my salary accumulated in my bank account in France while I was living extremely well on the expenses allowed for me in the States.

Every two weeks, I was sent to a new city and met with department store managers anxious to welcome me and show me their city. The name of Christian Dior opened doors throughout in the industry. My contacts took me out every night and if I was there on weekends, they would make sure I was never left alone. In Saint Louis, I even went boating on the Mississippi with a cousin of Rudolph Valentino. He did not look like the famous actor and did not have his apparent charm, but he was quite pleasant while showing me the sites along the great river.

Six months passed very quickly and all I could think about was how well-treated I had been. I was touched by the warmth, hospitality and friendliness of the people I had met. But the end of my diplomatic work was approaching and I had to get ready to go back home. A melancholy set in as I thought of leaving compared with the great joy I had experienced during my trip.

I needed more time to adjust to going back to France, so I exchanged my airplane ticket for a stateroom on the *Ile de France*, the most beautiful ship of that time. I promised myself I would never forget the land I was sailing away from.

The *Ile de France* was a magnificent vessel. Because of my brother's relationship with one of the executives in the company, my cabin was upgraded to first class and my name was even put on the V.I.P list. I had no idea it would give me so many privileges and fun private parties.

The first night, I was invited to a cocktail party in a special lounge just outside the captain's quarters, then I was given a table for dinner headed by one of the officers. Harry Belafonte and his wife were at the same table. He kept rather to himself but was very pleasant when addressed. Someone told me he had had a bad cold and was being careful not to strain his voice.

On the second day, I received an invitation to a "couscous party" in the captain's quarters. Twelve guests and officers sat on the floor around a large white table cloth and we were served by crew members dressed as Arabs. I could not believe my ears when I was introduced to the other guests. A stunning tall blonde, Barbara Hutton, was at the time between husbands but kept everybody's attention with her wit and verve. A beautiful dark-haired woman was introduced as being the heiress of a well-known soup company empire. I wondered what I was doing there, but obviously the fact that I worked for Christian Dior kept opening doors.

Champagne flowed all evening and I could hardly make it back to my cabin. At the end of the evening, when I light-heartedly complained that I had to walk a long way from my cabin to the swimming pool, one of the officers handed me a "passe-partout" key. He explained, "With this key you can go anywhere you want."

Giving me that key turned out to be the most delightful thing that happened to me that evening. For the following days, I played tricks on the staff. I would wait for a steward to get near a closed door, approach the door and wait for the usual comment, "Sorry madam, this place is restricted to the crew only." Then, very seriously I would take my key out of my pocket, smile at the attendant, open the door and smile again without uttering a sound. Nobody ever stopped me or had any question about the reason I was allowed to use a short cut or enter a restricted area. This was long before terrorism existed. It was a time when trust prevailed over fear.

During the time I spent in the States, I had been dressed by Dior and earned a great living, all expenses paid. I was welcomed and accepted with open arms and I felt respected. So, at the age of twenty three and just for the fun of it, I bought myself a mink coat, which created havoc in my very conservative family upon my return. But I felt on top of the world and I was going back to France a different person. I was ready to go back to the House of Dior and face my life in a positive way, ready for any challenges.

Looking back, I see that it was more than luck that guided my steps when Louise told me about the Christian Dior two-week opportunity to work. It was a turn in the road directing my life towards my destiny.

Chapter Seven

Going Back to France

After all that traveling in England and the States, I was back in Paris and the House of Dior. I was put in charge of the men's boutique to replace a manager who had been recalled by the army.

I accepted the position. I knew it was going to be an exciting place to work because of all the interesting people involved in this special little world. In addition to some of the European royalty, I had the pleasure to greet and talk to people like Leonard Bernstein, Yul Brynner, Elizabeth Taylor and Sophia Loren.

I found out quickly about many intriguing things that were going on, stories that would have delighted the gossip columnists.

One of our regular customers was a lady who was married to one of the most famous men in Paris. She was at least sixty-five and she had a gigolo, a gorgeous suntanned young man of thirty-something and she wanted him well-dressed. Of course, she did not want her bill to end up in her husband's account, so we had to create a special account for her and make sure no mistake was ever made.

Everything was going well until one of the girls working for me fell for the gigolo. The two started exchanging words and smiles behind the lady's back and after a while she realized what was going on and asked to speak with me.

"I have the power," she said gravely, "to have you and

your salesgirl fired if you do not put a stop to this nonsense immediately."

I excused myself and summoned the salesgirl to the back room. Shortly after that, the salesgirl graciously and thankfully accepted a transfer.

On another occasion, one of the greatest composers of our time also came to the shop. One day, he came by and insisted I help him choose his ties. As I was selecting suitable ties and conversing with him, he abruptly changed the subject and offered me a job. He explained, "All you have to do is travel with me and every now and then I will give you some work to do." Then he added with a smile, "You will earn a large salary."

It was difficult not to lose my temper, but somehow I managed to leave the room and cut short his explanation.

I was deeply insulted and embarrassed. But I had to swallow my pride. I knew these sorts of things were not uncommon. After all, the Dior staff were chosen for their experience, brains and looks. We were warned about situations like this and taught how to remain diplomatic. The key was to avoid displeasing a cherished customer, especially if, as in this case, that customer happened to be world-renowned.

This was a time when sexual harassment laws did not exist, so we were trained to manage on our own. Knowing what to do, I returned to the customer, delicately declined the offer and, after one of the other staff members helped him with his selections, wished him a good day.

It is unfortunate that power and money do not always go hand in hand with good education and respect for others. What became clear to me was that some of the wealthiest people in the world believed they could own anybody they chose just by asking. Fortunately, they were few and far between.

Twice a year, the real excitement was the unveiling of a new collection, when we would have a highly-anticipated fashion show The preparations never seemed to end. As the day approached, the dressmakers, models, accessory girls, managers, salespeople, public relations people and many others became super-energized. The house was like a bee hive. Very few people slept the night before.

The big day would finally come and the favorite buyers would take their assigned seats in the front rows alongside well-known personalities and actors. Those who were fortunate enough to get a special invitation to the Premiere would be assigned a seat according to their importance. The further away their seats were, the less important they were.

We, the employees, sat on the stairs, filling the huge staircase from the bottom up. Like our clients, we were arranged by ranks, with the directors and managers in front, followed by the best salespeople and public relations people. The rest squeezed themselves together on the top steps, straining to get a glimpse of whatever created the loudest applause. It was one of the highlights of working for Dior.

In the world of fashion, who you know is nearly as important as who you are. One day, we were told to expect a famous visitor, the head of the House of Hermès. Monsieur Guerant was a very important personality and I had not told my manager that he was a cousin. When he arrived I stayed pretty much in the background until it was time to introduce myself and then I did so with relish. He gave me a hug and told me to give his best wishes to my parents. I can still remember the look of shock on my manager's face. She had been making a big deal of this visit and the surprise of a subordinate's close relationship with Monsieur Guerant hurt her pride. For several days after that, she avoided me. I went back to work as usual thinking she was making a big deal out of nothing. But she told me later I should have told her beforehand.

What I would understand later was that people in the fashion industry, because of its superficiality, took notice of such details. It turned out to be much more important than I realized. In fact, I started to wonder if my relationship to the House of Hermès, which Mr. Rouet was aware of, had anything to do with the wonderful position I got as a Dior ambassador to the United States. I also questioned why I was given a new position immediately after coming back to Paris instead of having to wait for another trip abroad. Was it just a coincidence? I was young and naïve and didn't understand the politics in this huge company.

---⊗⊗⊗---

In my own family, my world seemed unbalanced. I felt like a misfit, totally misunderstood. My parents were treating me like a teenage girl and my brother and sister were not particularly interested in hearing about the U.S. I started to feel a calling to return to the land that had given me nothing but the best.

After one year of thinking it over, I told my parents that I made up my mind to go back to Chicago, because I was so happy there.

They were very sad when I shared my decision with them, but they reluctantly agreed. My father insisted that I accept a fully-paid return ticket to France. "Promise me you will use it in the event the United States does not turn out to be the paradise you envision." I promised.

I must have been either a disappointment or a mystery to them. Choosing an art school at fifteen in Paris, living in England at eighteen, working for Dior at twenty one and now, planning to go halfway across the world to pursue my dreams, it must have been a lot for my conservative parents. Traveling to a country as far away as the States was strange and not something they had ever envisioned for any of their children.

Years before, my father had traveled to the U.S. on one of the first liberty ships, which carried just a few people immediately after the war, to study a new type of electrical cable. We had been living with very limited rations during wartime France, so he was amazed at the abundance of food and other products there. He arranged to have a guide help him buy a trunk load of clothing and non-perishable food for us. When the trunk arrived, it was like Christmas. I will never forget that he brought me some beautiful shoes, which I tried and tried to fit on, but they were just too small.

Years later, when I decided to go there, he was probably afraid that he would lose me forever.

There was nothing my parents could have done to stop me. All I wanted was to go back to happiness and freedom, to the country I cherished so much. And to this day I am grateful they let me go, because if I had not gone I would never have become the person I am today.

I quit my job at Dior in Paris and said goodbye to my friends. Then I said goodbye to my parents. They let me go, hoping my instincts were correct and wishing me well. And then, despite being a little fearful about my future, I left France to start the rest of my life.

Chapter Eight

Returning to My Adoptive Country

Out of the many friends I made in the States, two played important parts upon my return. I had met my girlfriend Pat through her parents who were friends with some friends of my family. Pat was younger than I, but close enough in age that her parents, when they first met me, immediately thought we could become friends and introduced us. Pat would be a pivotal force not only in helping me get a green card, but she also was the one who introduced me to my future husband.

The other friend was Jack, a comforting young man who helped me through the difficulty of adapting to a new country. Jack was my first American boyfriend. I met him in Chicago and he made up his mind that he wanted to marry me. He even went as far as going to France to visit me and meet my family while I was back there. I was very fond of him, but I could not see myself fitting into his very conservative Jewish family. He understood and never pressured me.

When I arrived in New Jersey aboard the "Maasdam," one of the Holland America Line's ships, I was feeling a little apprehensive. But when I saw Jack, I felt reassured. He had made it a point of finding out about my arrival and arranged a business trip to coincide with my itinerary. Then he was kind enough to fly back with me to Chicago.

Pat's parents were away when I arrived and would not return for three months. So she suggested that I stay with her in their plush apartment overlooking Lake Michigan on Lake Shore Drive.

Pat could not stay home for even one night. She always had to be out some place. I liked her a lot, but we did not have much in common. When Jack and I arrived in Chicago, she was there to pick us up. After dropping off Jack at his home, she said that my relationship with him was not good enough for me and that I was too young to be tied down. She then informed me that she had made three dates for me starting the day after next. When I told her that I appreciated the help but would rather take care of my own private life at my own pace, she burst out laughing. She explained that it was a really big deal for her friends to have a French girl moving to the States, especially one who had worked for Christian Dior. No doubt she had described me in an exaggerated way, adding some of her own fantasies to the narrative, so it seemed like everyone she knew wanted to meet "the French girl." And she knew a lot of people, as her family was part of the Chicago elite.

The day after I arrived, while I was busy arguing with Pat about canceling my blind dates, the phone rang. It was andrew, my date scheduled for the following Friday. According to Pat's plan, the man on the phone was supposed to take me out to dinner. But being a man of action and not especially enthusiastic about going on a blind date, he was determined not to waste an entire evening with a stranger without first checking her out. So he told Pat he was not sure he could take me out on Friday as planned, that he had to go out of town on a business trip. But he said casually that he could take us both out for a quick drink that evening if we were up to it. He lived in the same building, so he could be right over. We hardly had time to fix our hair and change into more appropriate clothing when the doorbell rang.

Reluctantly, I went to the door to meet the stranger and be polite for Pat's sake. But my first impression of this tall slender man was that he was good-looking and had a devastating smile.

I would have been surprised to hear that I was one day going to marry him and become the mother of his children.

The three of us walked to a small but cozy cafe bar just around the corner. It was supposed to be an early evening, with one drink, but it became a lengthy one with quite a few. Pat left us and went back home as she had to work the following morning. Andrew and I stayed in the little cafe and talked for hours until quite late, or rather, I should say, very early in the morning.

We discussed and planned how I could get a green card. Laughingly, he said on that very first night, "Why don't you marry me? It would solve your problems."

Throwing back the joke, I replied, "Of course, I accept." He took me back to Pat's apartment and I thought I had found a fascinating friend who would take the place of a brotherly figure.

He had his own airplane and asked me two days later to go with him on an aerial tour of Chicago. I was thrilled. But my first experience with a small airplane would turn out to be scarier than I expected.

It was winter and the ground was covered with snow. After landing at a tiny airstrip, we walked around for a while. But it was cold and Andrew soon decided it was time to take off again. The snow was heavy and slippery, making it hard for the twin-engine Apache to take off again. When we finally lifted off, it was within inches that we cleared the trees. Only a skillful pilot could have succeeded in that difficult maneuver and I was impressed and felt I could rely on this new friend. I smiled with approval.

I think it was at that moment that Andy, as everybody called him, became interested in me. I showed him I could keep my fear to myself and remain calm and in control. But more importantly, I showed that I loved flying.

For the two weeks that followed, I spent time hanging out with my new friend while continuing my relationship with Jack. Never once during that time did Andrew ever show me anything but platonic friendship.

Nonetheless, Jack was getting nervous about Andrew seeing me so much. He knew him in the business world they both belonged to, but more than that, he knew of Andrew's reputation with women and that scared him. He told me about it, but I only laughed at him as Andrew had been a perfect gentleman with me. Then one day, without telling me, Jack went to see Andrew and asked him point blank what he had in mind concerning his relationship with me. I never knew what the answer was, but I can guess that the first thing Andrew told Jack was to mind his own business. He might also have been more reassuring, saying that he only had good intentions. In any case, this incident forced all of us to think carefully about what was going on and I could no longer hide the attraction I had for Andy. I told Jack that I knew I would never marry him, that I really liked this new man in my life and felt deep down he was not as bad as his reputation. The mask we had been wearing during those initial weeks came off when we faced the attraction we felt for each other. I was lying to myself that he was just a friend. From the moment I saw Andrew's smile I felt an attraction that I tried to ignore when we spent time together. When I finally faced the truth, I found myself in love and determined not to let anything get in my way. So I plunged into a delightful romance and ignored any signs that the relationship would be difficult.

Meanwhile, Pat had found a connection to help me get my green card without leaving the country. Thanks to my fashion training in Paris, I got a visa with the very special title of "Indispensable to the Economy of this Country" and was allowed to work as a fashion consultant for an upscale department store called Martha Weathered. The owners, whom I had met on my previous trip, sponsored me and gave me a wonderful position. Pat's parents would be back soon, so I looked for an apartment as soon as I was hired.

At the age of twenty-four, I did not fully appreciate how fortunate I was to have a great-paying job, an apartment, wonderful friends and, above all, a man I loved, all within three months of arriving in a new country. I am not sure I even acknowledged or thanked the universe for it. At the time, I thought it was quite normal and natural. I believed one could get whatever one wanted, just for the asking and without much effort. I was not spoiled, but I certainly had no idea what it was to have serious difficulties. I would learn later, when the time was right, that I needed to go through hard times to appreciate what I had and not take everything for granted.

I met Andy's friends and there was no question in everybody else's mind that Andrew was a playboy. In fact I was warned by more than one person. But I was sure this was just part of his past and I thought he loved me enough never to go back to his old habits.

As for Andrew, I was the answer to everything he thought he wanted in a wife. But did he feel the love I felt at the time? I was not sure. One day, in a restaurant, he bluntly asked, "What kind of wedding would you like?"

This was so typical of him. He was so sure I would say yes that he never even asked if I wanted to marry him. In a way it showed the trust he had in me. There were no games, but I did keep to myself some of my fears about his reputation and what the future might be for us. Despite these fears, in my mind there was no other choice.

When I told Pat's mother about our plans, she was one of the first to be concerned. When my future mother-in-law gave me some warnings of how difficult the men were in her family, I answered, "I would rather be miserable with him than without him." That was how strongly I felt. It was much too late to listen to anybody.

I apparently made the right decision because, despite a marriage that ended in divorce, I am grateful for the children I had with him and for what I learned from our relationship. He would become one of my master teachers and true soul-mate.

The word soul-mate is often misunderstood by people who think it is simply someone who is compatible with you. But in the spiritual sense it means someone who teaches you the most, someone through whom your soul can grow and learn whatever has to be learned. This process is often painful but necessary. My marriage with Andrew offered these valuable lessons.

Chapter Nine

Discovering Our Many Selves

Andrew's charm was contagious and it would be one of his biggest assets during his entire life. I could never resist it and it took me a long time before I expressed my opinions truthfully.

We were married in the summer of 1960 and we decided that the best thing to do was to have a wedding with family and witnesses coming in the morning for a small wedding ceremony and friends joining us in the afternoon.

My brother Roby was sent to Chicago to represent my family and arrived the day before the wedding. He and Andy immediately became friends.

As Andy did not want to be married in a church, he made arrangements to have a judge, a friend of his, marry us in his home. Ten of our closest friends and family joined us as we squeezed ourselves into an elevator up to the judge's apartment. None of us could remember the floor he lived on, so we went up and down several times before finding it. In a way, it was prophetic of how our marriage was going to be, lots of unpredictable ups and downs.

The ceremony was short but moving. When we left the judge's home, I was so happy that I could hardly contain myself. I kept smiling, not only to the people around me, but to the strangers passing by.

We chose Andy's apartment for the reception and let a

caterer take care of all the details. We received our friends with the usual champagne and delicacies, which turned out to be too much. But the party was a delightful gathering, with well-wishers celebrating our joy and happy that Andrew had found the right girl and tied the knot. He was thirty-one and I was twenty-four.

My parents had planned another party at their home in Versailles. So the day after our wedding, we flew to Versailles, where my parents were waiting anxiously to meet their new son-in-law for the first time. My mother fell under his spell right away and would remain loyal to him until the day she died. Even when I started to face serious problems in our marriage, she always had something to say in his favor.

The following Saturday night, a crowd of friends and family invaded our house for our second reception, which lasted late into the night. Everyone was curious to meet my husband, hoping to find out why I had chosen an American man. It did not take long for Andy's charm and sophistication to win everybody over.

We spent our honeymoon in Switzerland before flying back to the States. During that trip, I became aware of the difficulties between Andy and me that would eventually drive us apart. He made all the decisions about what we would do, where we would go and I went along with whatever he wanted to do. After all, we had only been married a very short time and I did not want to interfere or be argumentative.

Life with Andrew was exciting. He knew how to arrange great vacations in remote parts of the world. Flying in our private plane or in one that we would borrow from a friend, we visited the Caribbean often, sometimes alone and sometimes with friends. We did a lot of sailing as well and because of him, I learned skin diving, water skiing, skiing and how to pilot the planes.

But there were difficult lessons as well. For example andrew and his parents spoke German together and the sound of that dreaded language brought back painful memories. All my insecurities of the occupation reappeared and so did my nightmares. On several occasions I woke up screaming and waking Andrew, who reassured me and went back to sleep. Eventually the nightmares disappeared and I got used to hearing German spoken around me.

Andrew and I were like two ships traveling in the dark. We did not know who we were as individuals and had no idea who the other really was.

To the outside world it looked as though we had it all. We were successful in our careers, which demanded balanced, smart and creative people. But in our inner world we were dealing with problems born during our early childhood that led to both of us being insecure. As a result, we were both in need of constant recognition and reassurance of how great, smart and capable we were. It became a dangerous game between us, as the competition to be the best at everything took over the common-sense approach of being the best in whatever each had to offer.

If we had been a well-adjusted couple, we would have appreciated the notion that one could be stronger than the other in certain respects or tasks. We would have rejoiced in our differences and that would have made us stronger in the long run. But some couples, like us, never achieve this. In our lack of communication and understanding, we killed our chance at happiness.

A strong ego in one of the partners, coupled with an overwhelmed spouse who begins to feel inadequate or unable to stand up to the other, can make it impossible to express what they truly feel. The refusal to communicate these true feelings can become like a fence between the partners that eventually leads to a lack of understanding, solitude and despair.

Shakti Gawain, author of many spiritual books, wrote, "Within each personality are many sub-personalities, or selves. To better understand our own inner conflicts and inconsistencies we need to become aware of these."

Andrew mistook my insecurity for weakness and thought the person he married was different from the person who was living with him at the time. I mistook his insecurity for a desire to control me and often thought he was either ignoring or badgering me. In my search for Andrew's approval I demanded too much, resulting in my getting less and less. I was finally faced with real challenges.

Thus, the molding of a human being was in progress and the shaping of a new life had begun. I would later ask why the universe would give me a husband I adored but whom I would end up leaving with my heart broken. It would take many years of searching, but I would find the same answer over and over again, that we learn the most from the people who hurt us the most.

In difficult and sometimes impossible situations, a lesson must be learned. I discovered that what seems to be the worst situation in your life at the time may turn out to be the best situation for your soul and necessary for your evolution.

In *The Seat of the Soul*, Gary Zukav says, "Every experience that you have or will have upon the earth encourages the alignment of your personality with your soul..." Being hurt by someone you love creates strong feelings that force us to explore more and rely upon ourselves more. I found out that when I was in great pain, when I felt rejected and only when my heart was aching was I truly willing to do the work necessary to change my self-centered attitude and regain a positive outlook on life.

But until I would realize these truths, I would struggle with a difficult marriage the best I knew how.

I found myself pregnant early on and this did not help our relationship at all. I wanted support and felt I was not getting it. It was the sixties, when most women dealt with their pregnancies alone and men had little to do with it. But I felt very lonely. Before long, I quit my job at Martha Weathered and prepared for motherhood.

Andrew was fighting his own demons. His father was a brilliant pathologist who contributed to many medical discoveries, one of them advancing knowledge on the causes of senility. He never let his son forget that he was *only* a business man. I believe most of Andrew's life was a struggle to measure up to his father, even after his father was long gone. As a result andrew had a difficult time giving positive encouragement or compliments to the people around him. He never understood how valuable it would have been to us, especially our children, to hear how special they were to him.

The birth of our first child totally absorbed me. Little Philip appeared on the scene with flaming red hair and we thought he was the most beautiful and intelligent baby ever born. It was 1961, just a few months after the Cuban missile crisis. America was on the verge of war with Russia and I shall never forget the fear I felt while listening to President Kennedy's speech. Holding Philip on my lap, I started to experience the trauma of war all over again and wondered if we could really go to war with Russia. Thanks to our government and the path our President took, we avoided the war and life went back to normal. With little Philip, I felt blessed, happy and totally immersed in the joy of having this wonderful child to play with as much as I wanted. I was proud of him and envisioned a life of beauty and success for this extraordinary boy.

But a storm was brewing in my marriage and my happiness would not last.

I might have neglected Andrew by giving too much attention to our son. I might have spent too much time in France showing Philip off to my family. Or perhaps Andrew's philandering nature took over and he began to look elsewhere for company. In any case, this was a difficult period when my instincts finally told me the truth, long before I found evidence of his unfaithfulness. But having been brought up in Europe at a time when men often had mistresses, I tried hard to ignore the pain and went on without saying a word.

We left Chicago and moved to New York two years later, before our second child was born. On the night that Robin was born andrew was away on a business trip and nobody could find him until noon the following day. When he showed up at four o'clock in the afternoon he was the last one to know he had a son.

We did not have a name for a boy, as I thought we were having a girl. The nurses urged us to make a choice and we did not have a clue. But when I looked at my fighting newborn with closed fists and the body language of a fighter who had come through a difficult birth claiming the world as his own, Robin Hood came to mind. So Robin he would be. It is a wonderful name for him because in some ways he has the heart of Robin Hood. To this day, he never ceases to amaze me with his sense of duty and responsibility towards his fellow man.

With three men in my life and two little ones needing my guidance and love, there was no turning back. I put aside our marital problems and decided to make my marriage work.

A friend of mine gave me a book she said would trigger a turning point in my spiritual development. The book was called *The Mystic Path to Cosmic Powers* by Vernon Linwood Howard. The book helped me realize that it was up to me to make desired changes in my life and that I had the power to stop others from hurting me. All I had to do was to follow some guidelines and trust that I would be guided along the way.

Meanwhile, I had another distress in my life. I was thirty years old when my mother was losing a long battle with cancer. I went to see her about six months before she passed away and we both knew then that we would never see each other again. I will never forget the look of longing and sadness she had on her face when she said good-bye to me.

Fighting back my emotions and tears, I went back to the States to take care of my children and husband. Day after day, I waited for the dreaded news. I felt guilty, that I should have been with her, yet I knew my place was with my own family. So I went on, just waiting for the phone call. When it came, she had already been gone a few hours.

I was grateful that I had so much to do before leaving. I had to pack and fly out that night. But once I sat quietly on the plane, I was overwhelmed with the thought that my mother was gone and I would never again have the joy of seeing her with my two little boys, who she adored.

I arrived in Paris mentally and physically exhausted. I had

to compose myself to be able to face the next two days. When I felt strong enough, I asked to see my mother.

I thought it would be very difficult. But when I saw her peaceful face, looking as though she was sleeping and without pain, I fell to my knees and finally cried.

Then, an extraordinary thing happened. A feeling of peace and joy invaded me and I felt her strength flowing through me. In a flash I knew for certain that from that moment on I would be strong enough to make the right decisions and face the uncertainties of my life. As she left us, she gave me the most wonderful gift that I could receive and it was exactly what I needed at the time: The courage to face all of my life's problems.

This was a turning point that showed me a different way of thinking. It was as if I left the room a different person. I shed my shyness, insecurity and fears for a sense of confidence and certainty that I would know exactly what to do when needed. Of all the gifts I received in life, these were the most precious and important ones, given to me by my mother as she departed life.

Chapter Ten

Chevry, My Parents' Success

W hen we lived in Versailles, we led a city life. Our apartment was more than a century old and we all enjoyed the architectural detail of an older building. It was also quite large. The kitchen was over a hundred feet away from the dining room, connected by a long corridor. In order to keep the dishes warm as it was carried across the apartment, our food was transported in a special heated rolling cart.

Contemporary life was not easy in those old buildings, but my father had a lot of remodeling done and our place was modernized. The only thing I never got used to was climbing the three flights of stairs with packages or suitcases.

The apartments were considered some of the most desirable in town and they had a view of the Palace of Versailles, which was just a stone's throw away. As young children we were often taken to the gardens of the Palace to play and get some fresh air. But as the years went by, we all agreed we needed a week-end house.

After months of searching, my parents found a farm in the small village of Chevry. At first, we could not understand why they bought a farm. But we could see the beauty they had in mind when my father told us his remodeling plans.

The horse and cow stables would become the living room, which would have a huge cathedral ceiling. At one end, a curved staircase would lead to the upper floor bedrooms. A contemporary kitchen would be built in what was the old living room, keeping the old beams and an old stone wall to give warmth and character to the new kitchen. He described his plans with vivid detail and made us part of them by including our ideas. It took about a year to finish, but the results were worth the wait.

My parents kept many of the old structures intact. One of my favorites was the wine cellar. About one hundred yards away from the house was a concave building, half of which was underground. To access the cave you had to step down a stone staircase. The walls had been built with large local stones, making the cellar soundproof and cold. The people who built it must have known the best temperature for wine, because after checking with some experts, my father concluded this was just right for his own wine.

He did not make wine, but he was a connoisseur. He also knew all about cheese and coffee. Wine, cheese and coffee were a pleasure for him, a hobby. When it came to coffee, he used to give my mother points and rated every cup of coffee she ever made, which always annoyed me. To this day, I have never been able to distinguish a good cup of coffee from a bad one.

The village was small but located near the famous forest of Fontainebleau, which made the weekly trip very pleasant. The only problem was that when we returned late at night, we had to be wary of the huge wild boars roaming around. They often were hit by cars, which created havoc. Luckily it never happened to us, but due to the animals' unfortunate circumstances, very few are left.

The farm also had a barn that was left the way it was originally built. For many years we had ideas about what to do with it. But nobody could agree on how to remodel it. In time I moved to the States and got married, my brother and sister spent less and less time in Chevry and my parents lost interest in the project.

When they bought Chevry, my parents decided it was going to be their retirement playground and that is what it became for them after their children left. While my mother occupied herself with drawing and reading, my father started, with the help of a gardener, to plant fruit trees. As was usually the case when he had a new hobby, he learned all about it and he ended up growing some of the biggest pears I have ever seen anywhere in the world. Even the marvelous Turkish pears were smaller than the ones he grew.

My father was proud of his successful garden and spent hours working on it. It was a source of relaxation from his stressful job in Paris. In fact, he and my mother never missed a weekend unless a *force majeure* happened. I had the pleasure of joining them in the summertime for a couple of years after I was married, finding much joy being back there.

When my mother died, the life went out of my father. Her death was devastating to all of us, but especially to my father who did not do anything without my mother's approval and encouragement. He worshiped the ground she walked on and always thought he would be the first one to go. She was the artist and the creator and he was the engineer who made the plans come alive. So after she died, his joy of going to Chevry was gone. Only his fruit trees kept him going back for a while.

He finally decided to sell the place. When he found a buyer for it, he did not argue on the price. He just took whatever the buyer offered to pay. When we told him he was giving the farm away, I never forgot his answer: "It does not matter. There is no price for happiness. I would have spent twice what it cost me to fix Chevry because it was never a financial investment. It was where your mother and I learned to enjoy our time together, to play and to relax, away from the world."

It was then that I understood what my mother meant to him. He survived her for five years, but he never regained interest in anything, not even when his grandchildren tried to cheer him up. To him, my mother and her Italian blood were passion and life itself. When the outbursts ceased and calm set in, he could not stand the silence. He would sit in a chair for hours, without reading, closing his eyes and, presumably, wishing to die.

After Chevry was sold, none of us went back to see what became of it. Of all the properties my parents owned, this one had more meaning than any place else. It represented a sort of paradise which lasted only a short while, but it captured the soul of both our father and mother.

Chevry was a lesson for me, as it made me understand better the relationship between my mother and father. They were so different that I could not always understand what brought them together. What I learned from them is that without any great enlightenment or spiritual wisdom, they made it work. It was their choice. Seeing them together and observing how they reacted to each other taught me the difference between being in love and just plain loving.

In this new world of ours, too often we wait for the right person to show up, to hear bells ringing and feel we are in love. Few people are lucky enough to find that very special person who will make them feel this way. Oftentimes infatuation gets in the way and love does not last.

Looking back at my life I did not always make the right choices because I was expecting to hear those bells ringing. I believe we have to be ready for love, ready to love more, to understand more and to accept being loved, only then, we might get the love we truly want. But sometimes our own selfishness gets in the way and makes it difficult to get what we want.

Chapter Eleven

The Night I Cheated Death

It had started as a routine operation. After having been in pain for some time following an infection from an IUD a few years earlier, my doctor decided the best thing for me was a complete hysterectomy. It was the 1970s and these operations were common in the U.S. at the time, even though alternative treatments were used in Europe. I was thirty seven and my doctor assured me it was not a serious operation, that I would be back on my feet in no time at all.

After the operation, I woke up in a lot of pain. I did not think much of it at the time, as I thought this was part of the process. But that night and the following day, the pain increased. The nurses were busy and did not give me more pain killers when I asked for them. Apparently the nurses thought I was just another difficult patient.

On the second day, one insisted I get out of bed and walk. I told her I was not sure if I could. But she said she would follow me with a chair, in case I had to sit down. I forced myself out of bed and started to walk towards the door. When a shooting pain made me lose my balance, I turned around to find the chair to sit down. But it was not there. The nurse had not followed me and she persisted in arguing that I should go on walking. I fainted before hearing the end of her speech.

A few minutes later I was back in my bed, waiting for a doctor. My own surgeon was away, but another doctor filling in for him was called in after I fainted. As soon as he arrived, the nurse started to tell him what a difficult patient I had been, intolerant of any pain.

The doctor was young, but he knew something was obviously wrong. He shushed the nurse. "Before making any judgments," he said, "we should examine this lady." When he touched my back in the kidney area, I let out a scream that must have been heard in the next room. When he checked my temperature, it was 104 degrees.

Suddenly all hell broke loose. The nurse apologized and the doctor announced an emergency. Everybody started running and shouting. A gurney was brought in and I was speedily propelled towards the X-ray room. A short time later, I was informed that during the operation a stitch was placed by my urethra, blocking the flow from my right kidney, which had died in the process.

The doctors realized they needed an expert and called in a urologist who had me transported immediately to another hospital. He would personally take care of me from that point on.

The trip was short and my husband, who had been notified of the emergency, was there waiting for me. But there was not a single room to be had in the entire hospital. I was given a space in the emergency ward, which also happened to be packed with patients.

When my new doctor arrived, he and another doctor proceeded to ask me questions and ordered some tests. They were shocked to discover that not only was my temperature extremely high, I also had one of the worst urinary tract and kidney infections they had ever seen. I was very weak and their prognosis was gloomy.

The urologist was young, but he was highly regarded in his field. To my good fortune, he had been conducting experiments on a variety of drugs designed to combat infections. After an hour or two he came back with a possible solution for us to decide on.

He told us that my chance of survival at that time was not great unless I was operated on right away to repair the damage done to my kidney and bladder. "But," he added, "I think you are too weak to survive another operation while your body is fighting such a serious infection."

He told us of an experimental drug he was working on that could reduce an infection in a matter of hours. He thought it might work on me and make it possible to operate on time. The problem was that it had not been approved yet and still was at an early stage of development. We had to decide right away and would have to sign countless papers to agree not to make him responsible for any possible outcome. I looked at Andrew.

"Please sign, "I want the chance to see my children grow up." We agreed to let the doctor do whatever was necessary to save my life.

That night turned out to be a nightmare. In addition to being very sick, the bed was uncomfortable, I was in pain and the emergency room had some pretty traumatic cases. One woman was screaming so loud that it seemed she was being tortured. The woman in the bed next to mine had taken some poison to end her life and was forced back to life by the hospital staff.

But I made it through the night. The administered drug was working and I saw the early morning sun peek through a window. I was told that my temperature was low enough for surgery. What a beautiful morning it was.

The operation lasted about seven hours. When I started to wake up I could not believe the excruciating pain I was in. They had to turn me onto my side every now and then, despite the pain, apparently to prevent my lungs from collapsing from having had two major operations in such a short time. They could not sedate me anymore, as my body had taken as much as it could and they were afraid of losing me. Maybe there were other reasons, but the nurses had their orders and kept on turning me while I called them the worst of names. Between bouts of insanity, I started to realize I had made it through, I survived, I was alive.

It took a long time to heal and get strong, but I finally did. I filed a lawsuit but lost the case on procedural grounds. I did not have it in me to go on with litigation, so I let it go. It was emotionally devastating for some time as over the years I had to get follow-up surgeries.

The matter remained a lesson in letting go. I figured I was better off without having won a judgment because the financial hardships that followed motivated me to work harder as an entrepreneur. In the end, the string of events helped shaped my life and helped me grow, as all the others had.

I often think of the urologist who saved my life and, I wish I knew what happened to him. All I know is that he moved to another state. How do you say thank you to someone who, first, had the courage to use an experimental drug on a critically ill patient and, then, had to spend hours repairing complicated damage that a professional colleague had done out of negligence? I hope he knows I will never forget him.

Chapter Twelve

Every day in every way,
I am better and better...

Shortly after Robin was born, I started to have agonizing headaches. Sometimes the pain was so intense that I would lie down in the dark for hours, taking medicine that did not help, often crying and praying for the pain to go away. When my migraines came, I would have given anything to make them stop.

In the late sixties, no doctor truly knew much about migraines. They could only recommend shots of morphine when the migraines were at their worst. They often had their patients take pills, which turned them into sleeping automatons. I hated medicine to start with and when I realized how bad it was to feed my body drugs that impaired my judgment, I knew it was time to look for alternative methods of treatment.

It was the very beginning of such practices in the U.S., but alternative methods had been around for years in the Orient and Europe. I was interested in what other people thought and did in the rest of the world regarding health and religion and read many books on the subject.

One day, while I was driving and listening to the radio, I heard a commercial for a lecture about the Silva method, which claimed, among other things, to help people get rid of their migraines. That's all I had to hear. I was ready to try anything if I thought it would help. So, armed with hope, I showed up at the Silva lecture. After three hours, I was convinced that I should take the course for the following five nights. That decision and my determination to get rid of my migraines changed my life forever and would catapult me into what would be the greatest force and help I would ever receive.

For a long time to come I would use the Silva method motto, "Everyday in every way I am better and better." When I first enrolled in the class, I could not imagine how powerful this simple little phrase would be.

Created by Jose Silva and originally known as Silva Mind Control, this program has been recognized for helping hundreds of thousands of people to develop their minds using tools, or a series of techniques, to become more positive and gain better control of their lives. The method consists of special meditations repeated over and over with the aim of hypnotizing one's self. Visualization is the main tool, using an extremely powerful technique to help the subject believe that his or her particular goals will be achieved without a doubt.

We were taught to put ourselves in alpha, beta, or, with a lot of practice, theta states. These states of mind correspond to brain rhythm, or brain wave cycles per second. The beta state is the outer conscious level, when we are quite awake. Alpha is a state of relaxation, most of the time induced by meditation. Theta is like alpha but at a deeper level of consciousness. Another one, delta, is achieved when you are in a coma or put to sleep artificially.

On the third day of the lecture, sitting in the center of a row of students, I started to feel a migraine coming on. This was a bad time to leave the room and the only remedy was to apply one of the techniques I had just learned. As I started the process, I convinced myself that it could work. To my utter surprise, it did work when the drugs did not and I was able to stop the pain and stay in class for the rest of the day. I was encouraged by my success and plunged into the program wholeheartedly.

I finished the course with even more astonishing results. For our graduation, we were given medical cases with very little information about the patients, only their names, addresses and a small description of what they looked like. We had to detect what part of the body was not functioning properly. By concentrating deeply I was able to solve six cases perfectly. Out of eight given cases, this was a great success.

In the following weeks my level of awareness was so high that I was able to detect difficult situations through my meditation and concentration just as fast as I would perceive my thoughts. One day, coming back home, I saw a strange car parked in front of our driveway. It was late at night, in a secluded area with no other house in sight. I stopped my car, concentrated for a minute and suddenly knew for certain there was no danger, as I could sense in my mind two young people kissing. I drove up to the other car and, sure enough, two young people were seated in the car. The young man came out and apologized for blocking the driveway.

What an extraordinary feeling that was. Instead of feeling scared, by using the technique, I had learned I was able to know for certain there was no danger. I continued practicing the Silva method and eventually controlled all my migraines, until one day, they disappeared completely.

I was grateful to stumble upon such powerful techniques. Decades later, I still use it. Like many other things in life it is easy to get complacent and forget about working on getting better. But I always get reminded, when the negativity of my surroundings becomes intense and my energy level starts suffering, that the Silva method will help me heal.

For about a year I meditated every day on the members of my family, visualizing each of them happy and at peace. Whenever I had a strong feeling that I should leave Andrew, I projected a good relationship. I did not want to believe that leaving him was the solution to my problems. I thought perhaps I did not understand the answer correctly and so I went on projecting and imagining a better relationship. I believed a divorce was the worst thing that could happen to a family.

But life would teach me later that in some cases separation is the only way.

By this time we were living in Concord near Boston and Andrew was taking quite a few vacations by himself. As he was about to leave on one of those occasions, I pleaded with him to cancel his plans or take me along. I sensed in my heart that if he went without me, it would be the beginning of the end. But he left anyway, unaware of the impending storm.

A few months later, I broke out into a terrible rash. The doctor told me my nerves were reacting to a bad situation. The only bad situation in my life was my troubled marriage, so I accepted the fact that it was making me ill. Realizing this was the end of our marriage, I asked Andrew for a divorce.

But I was tormented. If our pain helps us grow, how could the universe make a better human being out of me and at the same time ask me to break my children's hearts? Only time would give me the answers and only years later would I know that I made the right decision. Again I was grateful because deep down, I knew with absolute certainty we were going to be all right despite the chaos.

This was the beginning of my entirely trusting my instincts. But it was more than that. It was as if I was being manipulated by a force stronger than my own will. I felt I only had to have faith, to believe in the universe. I had never experienced anything quite like it before and it was like taking a step into an abyss, letting go of my own will, relying on my inner power to make the outcome right. And it was the right thing to do.

Philip, who was thirteen at the time, had asked me if he could stay with his father. I agreed, as I felt he needed a father more than a mother at this difficult turning point in his life. So with a very heavy heart, Robin and I prepared to move to a new home forty miles away, in a town called Cohasset on the Boston seashore.

During the fifteen years Andrew and I were married, we had moved from Chicago to New York and then Boston and this was going to be another one of my numerous moves. To me, moving always meant a fresh start and the hope of better days. But this time I was on my own with my younger son and not much financial support. Since I wanted the divorce, I thought it was fair to accept whatever financial decisions my husband made. With my new beliefs and practices, I embarked on my own, unaware of what was required to live, but with the strong belief that I would always be able to take care of Robin and me.

It turned out I was right. The universe would always provide. I recalled a remark Andrew had thrown at me in a moment of anger, when he learned I wanted to go into business for myself. He said, "You will never be a business person and your business will fail in six months." It was the best thing he could say to me at the time, as that remark motivated me to prove him wrong. And in some ways it became an obsession.

The following few years were some of the worst of our lives. Andrew was hurt by my departure and he replaced me with a much younger woman who moved into his life and apparently decided to play mother to my children. I was hurt and cried a lot.

But I knew I needed to take hold of my life. So I made an effort to meet new people. And, without any background in sales or marketing, I decided to open a gift shop. This launched me on a path that turned out to be decisive in guiding me towards a career that would become crucial to my wellbeing.

—⚬⚬⚬—

I found a small shop for rent on a side street in Hingham, not far from the original Talbot's. Armed with hope and courage, I stretched some fabrics on the walls and painted, bought a few store fixtures, a table and a second-hand cash register and prepared myself for my first buying trip to New York.

People used to comment on my good taste, so I thought it would be easy to pick up objects that customers would love. But I found out the hard way that buying is an art. In time I learned that it requires knowledge of your customers, a great deal of psychological know-how to understand what people want and the ability to detect the trends of the time ahead of everybody else.

I decided to sell fabrics in my new shop, so I imported some from Provence, France. It was 1975 and the fabrics I selected were about fifteen years ahead of the fashion trend in the States. Pierre Deux, the famous French Provençal shop, did not open its doors in the U.S. till years later. Being in existence earlier would have help me promote my goods at the time. When the fabrics did not sell, I decided to make skirts and bags out of the colorful fabrics. This was the start of my first venture into designing.

I found a wonderful dressmaker who would later become a friend. Terry and I created our first design studio. Very quickly it turned out to be a great success and gave me the idea to re-explore the fashion world. After using up the fabrics from Provence, I started designing very simple tops and skirts and had them made out of fabrics from a discount store in Boston that carried European goods. This was the answer. French and Italian fabrics were better than their American counterparts at the time and my new venture became quite successful.

When I first started, I questioned my ability and the outcome of what I was doing. It was hard to discard the opinions of well-meaning people, but I knew the answer lay in not listening to them. Keeping my negative feelings away and acquiring a sense of certainty that I would succeed was what I needed.

I learned to trust my instincts more and more. There was no time for doubt. Armed with the tools of the Silva method, I entered a totally new path. Working through difficulties and getting better at solving them, I started to reap some great rewards and satisfaction. And I was on my way to becoming a fashion designer.

———

While opening my shop, the divorce proceeded with difficulty. The emotional path sometimes seemed more than I could handle. I meditated a lot but relief sometimes was slow to arrive. It was hard to forgive and let go of the past while making a living and starting a new life. Learning new ways to cope with pain was not easy, but it became easier with each new battle and peace eventually set in.

When I was young, I believed others should act according to what I thought was right. But I learned that as time goes by, people react differently according to many factors influencing their lives at that precise moment. It would take trial and error as well as experience before I understood others' perspectives. I learned that people under stress, including myself, do and say things they do not really intend to. The stronger the emotion I felt, the stronger my reaction. I would eventually learn that wisdom requires work, understanding and the acceptance of our own human failures. What makes the difference between people who navigate blindly and more awakened people is the awareness of their human weaknesses.

I do not think I was a very good mother to my children during my divorce, when they needed my help the most. But my choices were the best I could make under the circumstances and were often tainted by the feeling that I was drowning at times.

Fortunately, not all my relationships were painful. The small town I had made our home brought me some of the best friends I have in my life today. Here again the universe sent me the help I needed by giving me emotional support and friendship. One couple, originally from Europe, would become so close that I think of them as family. They have done so much for me and I feel even closer to them than to my own family in France. In fact, Nicole is like an older sister.

I also started dating again, although I was not ready to get seriously involved with anybody. My newfound freedom had taught me what respect was, so I knew that whoever was going to share my life would have to share some of my principles as well.

Chapter Thirteen

Sacha

She was beautiful and took my breath away the first time I saw her.

Sacha was eight weeks old when I brought her home and I could not wait to show her to the boys. She was a pure bred Siberian husky with parents who were both champions. Her body was a brilliant black with a few white spots and her intelligent face was mostly black, except for the striking white markings framing her dark brown eyes. But this was not the reason I fell in love.

A few months earlier, I had asked my husband if he would agree to having a dog in the house. He was reluctant, but he said that if I could find a dog that did not bark or smell, he would agree to it. I plunged myself into all the books I could find describing dogs' habits and their characteristics. Of all the stories I read about, only the Siberian husky neither barked nor had a bad odor. Except, of course, when they're wet. Armed with my research, I told Andrew that I would keep the dog away from him when he was wet and he finally agreed to let a dog into our lives.

During my youth, I did not wish for a dog. Growing up in an apartment, my parents never allowed us to have a dog and that was never a problem with me or my siblings. But when my children expressed the desire to have a dog, I started to think it would be a great addition to our family.

Before Sacha, we had had a bad experience with a German shepherd puppy. We had brought him home, out of pity, from a badly-run kennel in Vermont. When the dog was one year old, he became aggressive and started to bite people for no apparent reason. When he turned against one of the boys, I accepted the fact that he was mad and that we had to get rid of him. After talking to several people, everybody agreed he had to be put to sleep, as no one wanted an animal that was dangerous and unpredictable. This experience had left such bad memories that I could understand why Andrew did not want another dog. But all that was going to change with the arrival of the new puppy.

Fortunately, there was a breeder in Massachusetts not far from our home who had a litter ready to go. When he showed me the litter, there were quite a few to choose from, but only one was showing any interest in my presence. When she licked my hand, I fell in love with her.

Sacha was going to become the little girl I always wanted.

Her first night at home was hard. She missed her brothers and sisters and she cried most of the night. The little sounds she was making were not loud, but I could tell she was sad and lonely. There was no way I could have brought her into our bedroom, as Andrew made it quite clear that that was out of the question. But she adjusted. She was smart and learned quickly to get used to her nightly boundaries. At bedtime she was confined to the kitchen.

Everyone agreed she was gorgeous. When I took her out on her small leash, people stopped and talked to me along the way. They commented on her markings and her dramatic, intelligent eyes. Sacha would wag her tail the whole while, as if she knew we were talking about her.

After reading in a book that you can teach huskies to howl, I decided to teach Sacha how to use her vocal cords. Day after day I sat on the kitchen floor with her between my legs and before long she started howling. She was a fast learner and started responding to my howling with her own. Remarkably, she never howled by herself; she always waited for my signal to start our duo.

When she was older, Sacha rarely used her voice. Only once, when a stranger came to the door, did I hear Sacha growl and show her teeth. I wondered, was that stranger a danger to us? Was her instinct telling her something my husband and I did not see or feel? I never found out why the stranger came to our door, because he left shortly after he saw Sacha.

She used to love running free in the woods behind the house. Sometimes she would bring back a small dead animal and drop it on the back kitchen stairs. I tried to stop her from doing this but her natural instincts were too strong and I did not succeed.

She was devoted to me and the boys, but never paid much attention to Andrew. Just before our divorce, when things started to be hectic around the house, she developed a terrible habit of relieving herself in the doorway of Andrew's office. It was in a dark corridor and more than once he stepped into the mess. Needless to say, that it did not make things better. But I had little control over her at that time. It was as if she knew what was going on and was distressed with the circumstances.

So, when Robin and I moved to Cohasset, Sacha came with us. She used to love running free in the new neighborhood and my neighbors knew and loved her. When I took her to dog school, she followed my commands well and I was proud of the fact that she was one of the best-behaved dogs in her class.

But well-behaved and smart do not always go together. Sacha was attached to us, but she was also very independent. On the last day of dog school, there was a competition in which every dog was graded and given a ribbon according to its ability to follow commands. During the last exercise, Sacha refused to obey. She looked at me as if she was telling me she had had enough and would not be a puppet to please the crowd. She sat herself down and nothing could make her move. Obviously, we did not win, but I could not stop admiring her spirit. She understood very well what was going on and had decided she would not participate any longer.

When she was four years old, I went to France for the summer with the boys and left Sacha with Andrew. His girlfriend, who now lived with him, had always shown some interest in Sacha and I thought everything would go well. But while I was in Paris, I received a horrible telephone call from Andrew. Sacha had died.

Apparently, they had forgotten to give her the heart pills she desperately needed in the summer and she contracted heartworm. When they realized she was sick, they took her to the vet. But it was too late. She did not last long after that.

I never thought the pain of losing her would be so bad. I cried for a long time and felt like my closest friend had left me. The Silva method helped me cope with the pain and suffering. I visualized her being happy and peaceful. I visualized peace and happiness for us all.

But I still miss her every time I see a husky. I can still feel that pain. No other dog will ever replace her. In fact, I sometimes think of getting another one, but so far something has always stopped me. Perhaps I am afraid of getting attached.

Dogs can teach you a lot. I learned that Sacha's instincts helped her react in ways that I did not always understand. But I never questioned her sensitivity as it turned out she always happened to be right. She helped me learn to trust my own instincts more and more.

Chapter Fourteen

Morocco, A Thousand and One Dreams

My divorce was finally over and I had not had a vacation in a while. It was time for me to venture on my own and take a trip. Morocco, to me, represented a beautiful and interesting country where I could find embroidered garments and beautiful objects for the shop. So I signed up with Club Med and traveled to Agadir, on the west coast of Morocco, along the Atlantic Ocean. I arrived there one beautiful April morning for a one-week stay.

The whole Club Med experience was new to me. It took me a couple of days to adjust before I felt comfortable enough to join in all the activities, the singing, dancing and water activities like sailing and snorkeling. The food was spectacular and I had a hard time not over-eating three times a day. In time I started to relax and enjoy meeting people of all ages from all over the world. By the end of the week, I felt so young that I forgot all the problems I had left behind.

But I was there to work as well. On what I thought would be my last day in Agadir, a guide named Ahmed drove me to Marrakech to buy dresses for the shop. It turned out to be a four-hour trip each way, across the steep *Haut Atlas* mountains. When we arrived in Marrakech at the *souk,* or local market,

Ahmed suggested I cover my blonde hair with a scarf in order not to attract attention. I did so and we proceeded to the market.

It covered a huge area. I was totally absorbed in the vibrant colors of the garments and beautiful jewelry on sale. It was hard to make my choices and I was so fascinated by the exquisite artifacts that I did not realize when it became dark. I was a little nervous about the trip, as I was not looking forward to the long return trip over the mountains at night. Ahmed seemed eager to spend the night in the big city, but I did not know the town well enough to let him choose our accommodations. So we left Marrakesh at about six o'clock p.m., hoping to be back in Agadir by midnight.

Shortly after we reached the steep road leading to the mountain range, the car started to make some peculiar sounds. Ahmed tried to sound reassuring. "This is a very good car and you should not worry about a thing. We'll be fine." He added, "In any case, it is too late to turn back."

Just as we reached the top of the mountain, the car stopped. Ahmed first asked me to help him push the car and then he changed his mind. "I will sit in the driver's seat while you push in order to start the engine." After I protested, he let me sit in the car while he pushed.

The huge mountains and their shadows put my nerves on edge. I was scared and wanted this ordeal to end. After thirty minutes, while Ahmed pushed the car along a flat part of the road, the car finally started.

We made it back to the hotel by one o'clock in the morning without any more delays. I complained to Ahmed about his frightful engine problems, but he insisted that I was safe all along, as we were traveling in Berber country and the inhabitants respected human life too much to cause any harm to strangers. I was glad not to be stranded all night and had no interest in finding out how nice the Berbers were!

Back in my room, I reflected on what happened and felt very grateful to be safe. I had a strong feeling the universe was watching over me and a sense of thankfulness filled my heart.

That night I meditated and acknowledged the gift of protection that I had been given. I felt watched over and loved.

―∞―

The following day was my last day and I had my luggage sent to the airport in the morning with everybody else's. While waiting to go, I received a phone call from the airline. There had been a mix-up with my ticket and there was no flight for me to go back to Boston that day. Outraged, I went to the bar on the beach and ordered a fruit punch.

There were a few people I knew there, so I joined them and related the tribulations and fears I had the day before and the fact that I did not know what to do about getting home, now that my stay at Club Med was over. I was eager to get my luggage back from the airport as soon as possible, so I asked aloud if anybody was going in the direction of the airport and could take me there.

A few seats away a Moroccan man sat quietly, clearly amused by my narrative. Before anybody had time to respond to my question, he stood up and announced, "I will be delighted to take you there."

"I hope your car will not break down." I answered insolently.

With a mysteriously confident smile, he answered, "No, my car works very well and if it did break down, you can be sure, I would have another one brought to me in a matter of minutes."

We promptly started towards the door and paused in front of a gleaming late-model Porsche parked in the very place where nobody was allowed to park. I knew it was his before he opened the door and held it for me. I felt embarrassed about my rude comment as I became aware of his privileged status here. When we arrived at the airport, people who had previously paid little attention to me were now willing to help get my luggage and arrange for another flight out of Agadir. It turned out there was no flight available for a few days, so my stay was prolonged. While all this was going on, my new escort stood behind me.

I do not know if he was directing my flight availability behind my back, but what was clear was that the apologies from the attendants at the airport were too strong to be normal. Once back in the car, my first question was "Who are you?"

"I am one of the King's closest friends, an architect and as part of my service to the King I am modernizing the harbors of Morocco. In fact," he went on, "this is the principal reason I am in Agadir." Later I would understand why he commanded so much respect here, when I found out he was a prince and his face was as well-known as the King's.

Meanwhile, I was worried because I knew Club Med had no rooms available for the next few days and I did not know where to go.

"Can you tell me where I might find a hotel room?" I asked.

"That should not be too difficult." was his reply.

But it did turn out to be difficult. It was a holiday week and most hotels had been booked months ahead of time. We went to three places that I could afford and got the same answer. There just was not a single room available. Even with his influence, we got nowhere. So he offered an alternative.

"There is a bungalow reserved for me in one of the largest hotels. You can use it and I will move out and stay with friends."

When I protested, he insisted it was not a problem, as he knew many people in Agadir. I did not have much choice, really, as the only rooms left were the suites in the Palace Hotel, where the cost was exorbitant and one night was about the equivalent of what I made in one month. So, after some hesitation, we put my things in his bungalow and he moved out.

I accepted an invitation to dinner with him. As a gesture to honor his country and thank him, I put on a beautiful black and gold Moroccan dress I had purchased the day before. It was floor-length and buttoned in front from top to bottom, with gold embroidery on a black silk background. The gold matched my hair color and I felt comfortable knowing that it was elegant enough that he could take me to any sumptuous place he might choose.

We first went out to dinner and then to a nightclub where the owner ordered some people to move so we would have the best table in the place. After living in the States for so long, it felt unreal to see people being forced to leave their table for another human being just because of his preferential status. Everybody in the night club was looking at us, some bowing their heads, some smiling, others just greeting us warmly, including the people who had been moved. I felt like I was in a dream. My friend, as I thought of him by then, seemed totally unaware of all the commotion.

He talked at length about his country and people in general. Educated, artistic and intelligent, he had a simple way of describing events without seeming to realize how magnetic his presence was. He fascinated me as I began to fall under a spell. Everything around me was like a fairy tale. I felt like royalty and did not want to fight this wonderful feeling, even though it could not last.

I stayed ten more days and lived a thousand and one dreams during that time. We visited his friends, we traveled and we played with the waves in the ocean and raced his car on deserted beaches. At night, back at the hotel, we swam in the largest pool I had ever seen, while the sirocco wind blew its madness in our ears. We laughed so much I hated the idea of leaving. One of his friends, an Arab man who was married to a French woman, told me he was the most sought-after bachelor prince in the country.

One interesting adventure was a visit to see and experience what I call "the blue women." On the edge of town, on the top of a huge dune overlooking the ocean, a group of women wearing long blue gowns stood still, making high-pitched fluttering sounds with their tongues. The image completely mesmerized me. Never before had I heard anything like this. These incredible sounds felt like beautiful music and penetrated my whole being to a point that I knew I would never forget the experience.

He invited me to stay longer, but I declined. Common sense

told me I should not expect more from a relationship so disparate. Cinderella is a beautiful story, but I had been married to a Jewish man who gave me two sons and the Arab world could never be mine. When I left, I refused to give him my address. I boarded my plane knowing I would never see him again and had to fight my tears back.

Back in Boston reality set in and before long I was back at work trying to forget my amazing journey and an incredible man. I don't even remember his name. But I will never forget the magical moments I spent with him and the way he treated me. An extraordinary gift of joy was offered to me at a time when I was struggling to recuperate from the sadness of my divorce.

When I met this man, I was expecting nothing out of life. I just wanted to have a nice vacation by myself. But the universe was beautifully generous to me, giving me ten unforgettable days. I believe some of the nicest things in life happen when you least expect them. It happened to me. It could happen to anyone.

Chapter Fifteen

Boston, Newbury Street

A few years later, it was time for me to move my shop in Hingham to what I thought was the real world. So I picked Newbury Street in Boston as a trampoline to throw me into a fashion world that I would later find to be fierce, competitive, tyrannical and demanding but also extremely rewarding.

By this time I had started to truly regard myself as a fashion designer. My simple original designs had evolved into a complete line of fashion wear and I hired a full-time patternmaker. The business grew quickly, I wondered if I was ready for such rapid growth. Did I know enough about the business to move it to a different level? Not knowing too much can give you the courage to do a lot of things you would not do if you knew some of the risks involved. In any case, I was pushed by my own desire and ambition to prove I had talents as a designer and a business woman.

Moving from Hingham to Newbury Street was not easy. Known as the "Rodeo Drive of the East", this historic, famous street was like a bastion guarding its shops fiercely and rarely opening up a space for newcomers. The same merchants remained there for years and realtors told me my chances of moving there were slim. But months before, I had made up my mind that it was where I belonged and nothing was going to stand in my way. Day after day I started to drive up and down Newbury Street, stopping whenever I caught a glimpse of an empty space. But nothing was adequate for my business.

Relying on the Silva method, I started to use a certain visualization technique, seeing myself doing business inside a shop on Newbury Street. About a week later, one of my best customers came into my shop in Hingham. While I was telling her of my plans and difficulties finding an empty location on Newbury Street, she interrupted without explanation and asked if she could use my phone in the office. A few minutes later she came back beaming and told me I had an appointment with the owner of a large shop on that coveted street. He was in the process of moving his business elsewhere and nobody knew about it. She happened to be a friend of this man and had coincidentally heard about his plans when she visited him a few days earlier, when he told her he wanted to find a tenant as soon as possible without having to advertise.

I showed up on time for my appointment and marveled at the space. In the back of the shop, a huge staircase divided the shop in two. I could already see the models displaying my designs in front of an audience seated near the bottom of the stairs. The possibilities were endless. But I was anxious to know what the rent was. My shop in Hingham was $1,200 a month for a thousand square feet. This shop was twice as large and located on some of the most precious real estate in the fashion industry. My budget was limited, so I did not think I could afford such an impressive location. After sitting down and answering questions about my business, the owner of the building finally told me that he would accept $2,200 per month for the first year with a slight increase the following years. I was overjoyed and struggled to refrain from showing how pleased I was. We signed the lease the same day and said good bye, both happy over a perfect outcome.

This was no coincidence and I could sense magical forces on my side. I felt on top of the world. After redecorating the shop and doing some advertising, more and more people started coming in.

But I soon discovered that there was a difference between the shops doing business on the first two blocks of Newbury Street and the third block, where I was located. Clarendon Street, one of the cross streets, was like a river separating the high-end shops from the rest. I would have to move again sometime in the future if I seriously wanted to be recognized as a Boston designer.

I waited two years and then the decision was made for me when the building with my shop was sold and the new owner doubled my rent. On the other side of Clarendon street a shop very close to the Ritz closed its doors after fifty years. I made an appointment with the building owner the day after the tenants moved out. The shop needed a lot of work, so I had the advantage in negotiating a lease. Once again, I felt lucky and knew the universe was on my side.

I wanted my new shop to reflect my position as the newest dress designer in town. Being across the street from the Ritz Carlton and a few hundred yards from Boston Common, I could not have asked for a better address. My new store would have nothing but the best. The Moroccan trip was long forgotten, but it gave me a lingering sense of respect and yearning for luxurious items. With that in mind, I bought four crystal chandeliers at an auction and made them the shop's focal point. Everything was done in gray and white, reminding me of a Christian Dior Boutique. Within a month I was ready for the opening and proud of how the shop looked. It was elegant without being ostentatious.

In addition to my own designs I included garments from outside sources to meet growing demand. Despite the shop's early success, the burden of moving, remodeling and buying inventory was very expensive and I started to feel some strain in my finances.

I had had very little training in business and I went along with my fingers crossed, hoping that I could cover all my expenses each month. With two full-time staff members and a few part-time employees, I was conscious that I had never been responsible for the wellbeing of so many employees before. But there was no time for any business courses. I learned by experience.

Without realizing it, I had become an entrepreneur, with all of its excitement and anxiety. The glory was easy to accept as my name appeared in *The Boston Globe* and other local magazines. I also was interviewed on television by Sharon King, who had her own show at the time and the *Good Day Show.* During one television program, I was interviewed with another dress designer, Alfred Fiandaca, who famously designed for Joan Kennedy. From then on, I thought, everything was going to be easy. And it was, for a while.

———∞∞∞———

One day, while working in the shop, I started having terrible pains in my lower back and I had to lean against the wall to ease the pain. When I commented on it to a client who was shopping with her husband, she pressed for details. Destiny was on my side again because she and her husband happened to be doctors specializing in kidney disorders at Massachusetts General Hospital. I told them what had happened seven years before, when I had the surgery that nearly took my life.

After all those years, I thought that old trauma was forever finished. But here I was, seven years later, with a husband and wife team of specialists sending me right back to the hospital. They both followed me there and took care of me.

It turned out that having so many operations in the same place had created adhesions that were strangling the path to my kidney, making it swell like a balloon. After struggling to figure out a solution, a team of doctors and surgeons finally decided on a course of action and proceeded with an operation.

It took six weeks for my body to heal. I tried to run the shop from home with the help of a few friends, but being the sole buyer, designer and manager, my presence was crucial during this critical period. My operation happened in May, when I should have been traveling and selecting the merchandise needed for the fall season. Plus, my own collection was being developed and my patternmaker quit. When I recuperated, I fought for many months to keep the business going but just could not save the sinking ship. I eventually had to sell my lease, leaving French designer Guy Laroche to take over.

~∞~

But as always, when I was at an all-time low, I got help. Some friends suggested that I visit a spiritual man, some kind of a guru they knew by the name of Greg Tiffin. They always went to see him when he was in Boston and were so impressed with his wisdom that they insisted I make an appointment with him. I trusted their judgment and went to meet him.

Greg was visiting from Texas and would be in town for a few days. His *raison d'etre* was helping people understand their life lessons. He had spent seven years studying with monks in Tibet and came back with the ability to read people's minds and, more importantly, to tell them what they were here to learn in this life.'

When I walked into the room, Greg told me to sit down and be quiet for a while. Although he could not have known anything about me beforehand, he proceeded to tell me my life story. Then he told me the word that embodied my life lesson: ADAPTATION. He said that the changes in my life were geographic, financial, physical and, above all, emotional. He explained that those changes were all for my growth and were necessary to mold my soul.

The events of my life became clearer to me as he clarified why I went through so many ups and downs. But it was his last words that would resonate in my mind forever.

"It is not going to become easier. But as you are faced with more difficult tasks, you will be given the strength and the power you will need." He went on. "All you have to do is to trust that you will get the help you need and will be guided along the way." I left feeling more confident that I could cope better because I understood there was a reason for the apparent chaos in my life.

After I closed my shop, I had to face another difficult change. Robin asked about living with his dad and brother. Staying with me was not the best arrangement for Robin because he never liked the school he was at and he preferred a school close to where Andrew lived. So it made more sense to let Robin go.

After that, he and his brother came to visit me on Sundays. On the surface they looked well-adjusted. But both suffered from the divorce and slowly grew a bit more distant from me. It hurt to see them come for a few hours, not even willing to stay the night and influenced, I thought, by a dad who still had a hard time accepting that I left him. I started to think we would be better off if I lived further away from them so they would spend longer periods of time with me, while on vacation for at least one week at a time. Having them at least several days in a row would give me a chance to repair the damage.

A close friend, Jennifer, was moving to San Francisco at that time. She was going to get married and live there and she did not want to leave everyone else she knew behind. So it seemed that San Francisco was the answer. It was far away from the boys but readily accessible by plane.

I reflected on everything that had happened the previous year and realized most of my difficulties turned out for the best. I still had a long way to go to be content and at peace, but the universe was leading the way. Even moving twice on Newbury Street was the right thing to do, as I never would have gotten my last shop without getting the first one. And, despite the business closing, I knew my career would go on and provide well for me in due time. Plus, my health could have been much worse if not for the skill of a great team of surgeons recommended to me by the doctors who happened to be in my shop just at the right time. So, I had to trust it would be the same regarding my relationship with my children and the best was yet to come. I knew that it would be easier if I had a brand new start.

I did a lot of visualization on my sons, seeing them well and content and I worked on getting rid of any negative feelings I had towards their father. I knew with certainty they would come back to me one day with a better understanding of what had happened during their teenage years.

Chapter Sixteen

Mystic India

Closing the shop on Newbury Street was not the end of my fashion days. In fact it was the beginning. I had patterns made for my own original dresses, sportswear and an entire collection of evening wear. It was just a question of finding out how I could make all my hard work pay for itself. The retail business was not an option at that time and I was not sure what to do next. But I knew my collection was valuable and I could sell my designs.

As usual, help came a few months later. This time, it was in the shape of a woman from Texas who had been in the fashion world for years. Her name was Bea and I met her at a cocktail party. After hearing about my circumstances, she became so interested in my story that she asked for a meeting the following day. When we met again, Bea convinced me that we were an ideal team and she wanted to enter into a partnership. I would be responsible for all the creations and she would do the marketing in Houston, her hometown, where she knew a lot of evening-wear buyers.

"Arlette," she added, "I know India well and have plenty of connections there. It's the ideal place to go for brocades and silks and you could go and get everything you need for your evening wear.

From what I had heard from Bea and other designers I knew from the trade, this was the right thing to do. "I think you're

right, Bea. India does have some of the most exquisite fabrics."
We were onto something that would be quite profitable. "You
know," I went on, "I could also find the right labor force to
make my dresses."

The opportunity was too good to pass up. Feeling quite
excited about meeting this new challenge, I accepted it with a
great deal of enthusiasm.

Once on the plane, the realization of what I was doing hit me
hard. India might be a wonderful adventure, but it might also
be very difficult as I would be on my own, miles away from
anybody I knew, with only the help of a few people Bea knew
there.

I arrived in New Delhi at one o'clock in the morning after a
day-long trip from Boston. Nothing prepared me for the cultural
change I encountered. At the airport, people were sleeping on
the floor everywhere, directions were hard to follow and the
accented English was difficult to understand.

Going through customs, an officer confiscated my curling iron.
I never thought, especially at that time, that my hair apparatus
would be taken for a weapon. Fortunately, Bea had arranged
for a driver to pick me up. He convinced the customs officer I
was a famous dress designer who had only the best of intentions
regarding India and that the officer should give me back my
curling iron immediately. The driver looked disapprovingly at
the officer, reflecting how he felt about the way a privileged guest
was treated. The officer hurried back with the object in question
and apologized profusely for having disturbed me. This was my
first experience with authority in that country and I discovered
that how you communicate was key. It was all in the tone of
voice and volume. The one who spoke the loudest prevailed.

I thanked my driver for getting involved with the dispute, but
I was tired and hardly talked to him on the way to the Oberoi,
the best hotel in New Delhi at the time. I would stay there until
I could find a less expensive home for my three-month stay.

The day after I arrived, I made phone calls and tried to get organized, but soon had to face the fact that efficiency was very elusive in India. "Immediately" could mean a week or more and "today" could be anytime between now and the following three days. As I did not want to stay in India more than I had to and was in a hurry to find the right people to sew my dresses, it was difficult to stay calm and relax. I tried hard not to let the delays upset me.

I had been warned ahead of time about the difficulties of doing business in India and it was just a matter of time before I would learn to play the game. All I had to do was get used to new ways and adjust my thinking. After all, I was in a country very different from my own and it was up to me to adapt to their ways. During all the negotiations, what struck me the most was the politeness and the good will of everyone involved. Even in a disagreement, the tone never became disrespectful and our rapport would remain this way during my entire stay.

While at the Oberoi, I dined in an opulent dining room and had the most wonderful five course dinners, including wine, for only ten dollars. It was good to know my money would go a long way in India, about five times further than in the U.S. But I had to be realistic and find a more reasonably-priced place for the coming months.

Within a week, I found a delightful locally-run hotel in a small, ancient palace recommended to me by some American diplomats I met at the Oberoi. The Claridge was the place to go for long stays. I was given a huge room, maybe forty feet square, with a balcony overlooking a garden of flowers and I felt thrilled by my good fortune. The cleanliness of the room impressed me, especially after I saw the chamber maids using brooms instead of vacuum cleaners to clean the carpets. They also changed my sheets every day.

When I left the States I had been warned by another designer to avoid the outside world during the beginning of my stay. She used to go to India on a regular basis.

"If you start to react to the overwhelming poverty there," she informed me, "you will not be able to stay there for any length of time."

Taking her advice, I started off concentrating only on places to visit as a tourist and to work, taking taxis everywhere I went. Later, when I took the time to look, I was grateful for her advice.

I will never forget the sight of little children who were mutilated, exploited by unscrupulous people who cut off their fingers so tourists would be more sympathetic and give them more rupees. Feelings of helplessness invaded me often, knowing the world around me was so dark for some people and I could not do much about it. I went around with quarters in my pocket and gave as much as I could, knowing quite well I would not change their lives, as the money would probably end up in the wrong pockets. The sight of such poverty made me feel guilty to have so much and I learned once more to appreciate what I had.

It is in India that I took my first steps towards enjoying the present moment and not always focusing on the future. I met a few Buddhist people who helped me understand the futility of planning for tomorrow and I was able to enjoy each hour as a gift without worrying about the future.

I was lucky to meet a great guide to help me buy fabrics. Shantra was a sophisticated lady who had known some better times, having come from an aristocratic family in Burma. She had an excellent knowledge of the area merchants and was quite an asset in my new venture. She also would become a friend.

One day, we decided to go to Old Delhi to buy brocades in a special place she knew about. This part of Delhi was different from New Delhi, as no Europeans ventured there. You could not go by car or taxi and the crowds were so dense that you sometimes had to push your way through or step over the body of some poor soul lying there. We were able to find a rickshaw driver to take us part of the way but had to walk at the end, where we found ourselves in a living sea of humanity, packed together and rendering the trip impossible to proceed on wheels.

As we were walking, I was amazed by the consideration

and respect people were showing me. Was it my European appearance? Did I behave differently? Or was it the fact that I was a woman? I did not know then but would later find out, women who break the normal rank of their usual duties of raising children are regarded as superior and, therefore, highly respected. I can remember an old man lying across the sidewalk who quickly scrambled aside to let me pass, saluted me in the most respectful Hindu way and blessed me at the same time.

Not only was I not afraid, but I was so well-treated by these strangers, that I felt secure in an otherwise insecure world. They believed in treating people with respect and consideration without jealousy, regardless of how little they had. What a wonderful lesson it was; instead of being envious or bitter, the ones who had the least elevated their souls by showing love.

We made it to our final destination and found ourselves in front of stairs so steep there was a rope on the wall to help people climb. There was chatter and we heard the sound of people arguing before we opened the door. When Shantra and I entered the room the noise stopped and a heavy silence fell. We had called ahead of time to announce the visit of an American designer but did not say it was a woman and the men inside the shop were surprised to see two females entering the shop. As custom demanded, we took off our shoes and walked on a floor covered with white sheets. The owner made a special appearance to talk to us and to bring me a chair, which was an exceptional gesture, as the other customers were squatting on the floor in the typical Indian way. We first talked about my stay in India and then about our families, until we finally came down to business. I had learned it was inconsiderate to start talking business without first attempting to get to know the other party and inquiring of the wellbeing of their family.

After I spent about one hour selecting the finest silks, the owner asked me if I would do him the honor of trying on a dress that he had bought from an Indian princess not long before. He said that the dress was regarded as a piece of art and I might be interested in buying it. After checking with Shantra, I agreed and retired in the back to change. I was not prepared for the beauty of that garment. The workmanship was exquisite and large pieces of real gold were sewn all over it in the most beautiful array I had ever seen. I put the dress on and walked back to the shop where I was greeted with strong applause. To this day, I still regret I did not buy that treasure. The price of five hundred dollars the owner wanted seemed like a very small amount for what it was. But I said no, afraid that if I bought it, the price of the fabrics I was purchasing for my designs would go up in the process.

India was a place of extremes. I was confronted daily with the abject sight of decay, ruins and the filth of poverty on the one hand and the sublime sight of magnificent palaces, art and unsurpassed workmanship on the other. The people reflected the same extremes. Some took advantage of the poorest people, lying, cheating and conniving to further their personal goals and some, often the most humble, left me full of admiration and awed by their spirituality and faith. Evident throughout was the affluence of the upper classes in contrast to the poverty of the outcasts.

An American woman I met, living there with her family, told me they were having a hard time deciding if they should ever go back to the U.S. Her husband was working as a drug enforcement officer for the government and did not make much money. But they had a life in New Delhi that allowed them to have nine servants to help around the house and she admitted that it would be hard to go back to doing the cooking, cleaning and gardening herself. A small part of the population claimed the right to have others pamper and serve them as slaves would do. The poor had no choice but to accept any type of work for measly wages.

One night, I received a phone call requiring my immediate attention at the factory where my gowns were being made. It was eleven o'clock when I arrived. I knew men were doing the sewing, but I was not aware that they were working twenty-four hours around the clock. The sight waiting for me was appalling, as half the crew was working while the others were sleeping on the dirt floor in front of their sewing machines. After taking care of some minor details, I asked to talk to the man in charge. When I expressed my horror at seeing the conditions these men were working under, I was told "Do not worry, they are happy and grateful for the work you provide. And in any case, I will treat them all to a movie when they are finished."

When I asked more questions I found out these men were getting one dollar a day but were happy to have the work and, as I passed through them on my way out, they saluted me with respect. I also found out that a quarter was what a lot of Indians earned for a day's work. A sense of guilt invaded me when I realized my dresses would be sold for many hundreds of dollars and the women buying them would never know the hardships involved in producing them. At the same time, seeing these men so happy to have the work helped me forgive myself.

My anger then turned to the owner of the factory, who was getting so much money from me and was paying his employees so little. But it wasn't worth a confrontation; this was the way that country worked and in any case I had a contract.

———

At the hotel, I met an English reporter who expressed her desire to go with me to Agra to see the Taj Mahal. I gladly accepted and we hired a driver for the day to take us there and back. It was a four-hour drive on dirt roads full of pot holes. The journey turned out to be quite an adventure and gave us a clear picture of this part of rural India.

On the way, we saw a dead man lying in the middle of the road and told our driver to stop. But he categorically refused. "It could be a trick to attract attention and I am not about to be the victim of bandits." he uttered in a low voice. So we asked him to go slowly around the body to make sure the man was not alive. We were convinced he was dead when we saw flies on his face. We could not say a word for the remainder of the trip. The sight of death meaning so little was hard to take.

We arrived at the Taj Mahal around noon. When I first saw it, goose bumps sprang up all over me. No photos or movies could have prepared me for the sight of that famous monument.

The long water-basin in front, the whiteness under the full sun and the shape itself made it breathtaking. As we approached the main structure, we saw the details of the mosaic made of semi-precious stones encrusted in white marble. The famous mausoleum was built by Shah Jahan for his favorite wife. It was said that he did not want any replica ever made and had the hands of the workers cut off after they were finished. Here again I was faced with the abject reality behind a most exquisite sight. After taking a lot of pictures, including some from the inside, I noticed a sign saying people taking pictures of the inside of the tomb would be prosecuted. I quickly walked away, hoping nobody saw me while my mind filled with images of an Indian jail.

Leaving Agra in the evening turned out to be difficult, as the bridge we had to cross was full of people, cars, bicycles and cows. Sacred cows abound all over India, but on that little bridge their horns looked twice as big and twice as sharp as usual. We closed our windows and our car crawled to the other side very slowly. My friend and I were glad we made it without incident. Four hours later we found ourselves safely back in our rooms at the Claridge.

My good fortune placed me in New Delhi in time for the *Beating of the Retreat*, a ceremony in which bands from the armed forces march and play music to signal the end of Republic Day celebrations. I was invited by the family of the Brigadier General who was in charge of the event and was told I would have a reserved seat to watch the parade. I knew it was a great honor and was thankful I did not have to be part of the multitude of people who crowded the parade grounds for those two days.

The general was a descendant of courtesans from the court of the Moguls in Agra and was a true *blue blood*. Being a Gandhi follower, he let his daughter marry a man from a lower caste who was the owner of the manufacturing plant where my dresses were made. So, with luck on my side, I found myself sitting a few rows behind Mrs. Indira Gandhi. What a privilege this was, to be so close to one of the most prominent figures of that time. She was dignified and she inspired respect just by looking at her. I was so thankful to be part of all this.

The parade started with jet planes spiraling down from the sky just over our heads. It was quite scary and I believe their flight path would never have been allowed anyplace else in the world. The parade went on for several hours and ended with extraordinary lights and fireworks that made the entire display seem unreal. The band ended with Mrs. Gandhi's favorite hymn, *Abide with Me*. The scene was spectacular and moving, as many thousands of people stood up and became completely silent, listening to the music in deference to Mrs. Gandhi. I was overwhelmed by the splendor of it all. With the multitude of people around me, as the music was playing, the sensation of it all was so powerful that I felt as if I had been transported to a church in the middle of nowhere, with a sense of peace I had not known. Never before or after in my life can I recall having had such a strong feeling of everything being perfect around me. When the music stopped, the noise from the crowd startled me and I quickly came back to reality.

I was driven back to the hotel in the general's car, ornamented with a dozen or so flags. I wished the vehicle had not created such a spectacle upon my return. I knew I would not forget that special day and, I thought, neither would the doorman of the Claridge, who was apparently very impressed with the huge limousine and all the flags.

Two months after arriving in India I became very sick. I had fainting spells and became very weak, so I went to see an Indian doctor who told me I was completely dehydrated. He recommended drinking a gallon of water when I return to the hotel and going on drinking three times as much as usual. He added that many foreigners have the same problem. They don't drink enough in the heat because they only drink bottled water, which is not always available. The fear of not finding a clean bathroom at the right time also inhibits many foreigners from drinking enough.

About one month later it was time to leave. It was also time to make sense of everything I had been through in India. It was at that point that my perspective on what was important in life changed forever. I could never forget my experiences, or the injustice and poverty I had witnessed. It taught me to concentrate on the blessings I had in my life. With this fresh new outlook, I departed a country I would never see again.

I believe that you can better appreciate what you have when you have seen immense poverty, disease, injustice, lack of sanitation, death and children having been maimed and abused by adults. I also believe you can learn from the resignation of the poor, who go on their way without envy or jealousy of the more fortunate. India taught me humility and gratefulness for the blessings I have in my life. It renewed my appreciation for my adoptive country, which received me and let me have the freedom to be who I am and want to be.

Back in the U.S., I waited for the gowns to be shipped to Texas, where Bea would market them to local buyers. Of course, the dresses were late. We just had to be patient. I figured that after my trip to India, the hardest part of the venture was over. But about one month after the dresses arrived and we signed a lease on an office in downtown Houston, Bea succumbed to a heart attack. She was getting ready to go out that night and she fell to the floor and died immediately. Her family was devastated.

After her husband and I recuperated from the shock, we had to face the fact that our investment was at risk. I was not familiar with wholesale marketing and it looked like Bea's husband and I would lose it all. With one hundred gowns on hand, we decided to split them in half to try to liquidate what we could and salvage some of the capital. My half of the gowns would be stored in Houston until I knew where to have them shipped.

The office building owner was quite sympathetic to our loss and easily canceled our lease. I went back to Boston and prepared for another beginning, my move to California.

Chevry

Couscous party in the Captain's quarters

Sacha enjoying the snow

Robin's high school graduation

With Fiandaca and Carol Nashe on national television

In front of the Taj Mahal

Part Three

Chapter Seventeen

Moving to California

Just before the summer I found a house in Mill Valley that was available to rent for two months. It was a short ride to San Francisco and my friend Jennifer went to see it and told me it was a charming house. Upon her recommendations, I leased it without hesitation.

I had decided to take my sons along and make a camping trip out of the journey. My car was a small Alpha Romeo Spider and was not big enough for the three of us, so I decided to get a larger vehicle and looked for a student to drive the Spider across the country. Quite a few people answered the ad I placed in the Boston Globe and after choosing the best applicant, I concentrated on buying an old Volkswagen bus to be our transportation for the journey ahead. My plan was to sell it once we arrived on the west coast.

As I did not want to sleep with the boys in their tent, I found my new bus to be perfect for piling up all my clothes in the back and putting a mattress on top, where I would sleep at night. It made a comfortable bed, but my many outfits would need a good pressing upon arrival.

There was also enough room to bring along our camping equipment, a tent for the boys and cooking apparatus for me, as I was determined to learn to cook outside and live under the sky for a while. I made sure I had a folding chair for the times I would not want to sit on rocks and dirt. So we left, excited about this new adventure and ready for the long drive ahead.

When we stopped at different campgrounds, I noticed my sons enjoying the camps even more than the trip itself, talking to people and making friends with perfect strangers. I was happy to see that such an adventure was bringing us closer together. We did a few side trips to explore unknown areas, taking turns driving and resting.

Five days after we left Boston, we reached the Rockies. We spent the night in Boulder, Colorado and felt ready for our mountain crossing. Mentally ready, that is, but ignorant of what was waiting for us. Our bus was loaded to the maximum and nobody thought ahead of time about the steep mountain roads. We got halfway to the top without any problem. Then the road made such a sharp incline that, when I saw a ranger along the way, I stopped to ask him if he thought we could make it to the top. Looking at our crowded Volkswagen, he had a skeptical smile and answered, "I really don't know. But if you break down, we have rangers closing the roads at night and they can rescue you." He pointed out that since we were already halfway there, it might be all right for us to go on. With great hope but less confidence, we started up towards the top, stopping at intervals to let our car cool down and to admire the breathtaking view of our surroundings. Sometimes two of us would take a walk along the steep passages, leaving a driver to steer the car. I kept thinking about how I did not want to get stuck there and hoped German car makers were as good as their reputations.

We reached the top very slowly and got very excited when we saw the sign telling us we were at the highest point in the Rockies. We stopped to take pictures of the snowy mountains and shouted out how beautiful it was as we felt relieved of having made it. The air was so pure and the sight almost unreal. It was exhilarating. We took our time before going down and I felt thankful we were able to drive our bus so far without incident.

Towards the end of our journey we stopped in Reno, Nevada. It was quite a new experience to see a gambling city. In a drugstore, Philip saw a gambling machine and threw a dime in it, never expecting anything to happen, but the machine spurted out lots and lots of coins. I believe it was beginner's luck, as it never happened again. Philip was turning twenty-one, but Robin was only nineteen, so he was told he could not play any of the machines. But to his satisfaction, he was allowed to come inside the casinos as he was accompanied by his mother. We had fun playing the coin machines and were lucky we did not lose more than a few dollars.

Philip and Robin had a birthday coming soon, so I asked them what they wanted. Both answered they wanted cowboy boots. This was the perfect place to buy them, as many shops offered lots of choices. After looking at several places we finally found the right boots. So, outfitted with their new purchases, the boys and I left Reno with good memories and eager to reach our destination.

We arrived in Mill Valley in the middle of the day and were happy to see that the house I rented was as charming as Jennifer had described it. What delighted us even more was the hot tub in the garden behind the house. It did not take long before we all jumped in.

Shortly after our hot tub dip, we were graced by visitors with long antlers walking through the yard. These deer became our friends and it always amazed me to see them come so close to the house. We just had to make sure the doors were always securely locked so our four-legged friends could not come in.

Having both my sons for a while was such a joy that I felt the time going too fast and I dreaded to see them leave. I had missed them terribly. This vacation was full of memories that I would need in the days ahead, when loneliness would set in, after they left. It had helped patch some of our differences and I was glad of the decision I made to move away from Boston.

While they were still in Mill Valley I answered the phone one day and found myself talking to a nice gentleman who, although a friend of the owner, did not know she was away for the summer. A few words led to a long conversation and before I knew it, I had accepted an invitation to lunch from a complete stranger. He was in town for the day, visiting from up the coast in Mendocino and he did not want to have lunch alone.

After I hung up I rushed back to my sons and told them what happened, wanting to know what they thought, hoping deep down they would tell me to cancel my lunch. To my surprise, both at the same time told me they would check him out when he came to pick me up and then Philip added, "You don't know anybody in California and this is just one way of meeting people." I always loved the directness of my two sons. They had had to mature fast and the result was they were always matter-of-fact, honest and not afraid of saying what they thought. So I felt reassured enough to get ready for my blind date.

When the doorbell rang I was pleasantly surprised to open the door to a good-looking, suntanned, fiftyish man, with a large grin on his face. Gerry, as he introduced himself, immediately proceeded to tell me how lucky he felt that I accepted his invitation. A flow of compliments followed. Welcome to California and its make-believe, I was thinking deep down. This man was a true representation of what that youthful state was all about. We were going to become good friends.

After Philip and Robin left, Gerry invited me to visit him in his home in Mendocino. He wanted to show me his huge house, built on the requirements of his ex-wife, who happened to have been Lee Marvin's first wife. Before long, after she married Gerry, she started to miss her Hollywood friends and went back to Los Angeles, leaving him a house that was more a theater than a home.

California was a new place for me and I often felt lonely. Gerry made me feel young and alive when I was far away from the family I missed so much. I believe he was in my life at a difficult time to help me and teach me how to laugh again. We had a great time together and I spent more and more time with him in Mendocino. But at that time, neither one of us could have imagined the traumatic experience we would go through together, in that house, in the near future.

Chapter Eighteen

Five Armed Men...

As the door slammed and the screeching sound of tires faded away, Gerry uttered the first words. "How badly are you hurt?" Without waiting for an answer he added, "I think I can get loose from the ties." Upon getting my assurance that I was all right, he freed himself, untied me, went to an upstairs bedroom, found the only working phone, called the police and came back downstairs. When he looked down at his shirt, he saw a growing blood stain and all of a sudden realized the blow he had received earlier was not a punch but a knife wound close to his heart. All his strength left him and he passed out.

Too shaken by the events which just happened, I could not move for a while. The sight of Gerry lying on the floor made me snap out of my lethargy. He needed my help and I forced myself to move. I went to the kitchen to fetch some ice cubes and brought them back to put on his forehead. The front door flew open and the first police officers entered the living room. The detective in charge took one look at us and called the hospital.

While waiting for the ambulance to arrive I was inundated with questions that had to be answered. I had been too traumatized to want to recall the events of the past hour so soon and could only utter a few sounds. So, the police officer asking details about what happened, assessed the situation and decided to postpone his questioning until one of us was able to answer coherently.

On the way to the hospital I took Gerry's hand and squeezed it gently. He looked at me with tears in his eyes. He could not speak but attempted a smile reflecting what I also felt at the moment; we were glad to be alive.

The hospital was a small country facility. It did not often get emergencies such as this one. They let me stay with Gerry, who did not want to let go of my hand, as if I was giving him the air he needed to breathe and the will to stay alive. I ended up with him in the operating room and was bracing myself to have the courage to stay, when a nurse looked at me, dragged me out and took me to a small waiting room.

I always hated the sight of blood. Many years before, as a teenager, I had to help my brother save our mother's life after an accident that left her bleeding for hours, in the middle of the night, in the small town of La Rochelle on the French Atlantic coast.

My mother recovered, but the memory of all the blood she lost was etched in my mind. On this warm August night, so far from France, so far from my family, caught in a dramatic web, I felt like I was dreaming and none of what was happening was real.

As I was drifting away and falling asleep, someone came to tell me that Gerry had been operated on, that he was well and that the surgeon found out the knife blade had missed his heart by two inches. Shortly after, the detective came back and told me it was time to take my deposition. He was apologetic but firm, so I followed him to a private room where he made me sit down and recall the dramatic details of this night of terror.

The evening had started peacefully. Gerry and I had gone to see a play at the Mendocino Theater and, driving back to his house, we felt happy to be together. We both believed in the philosophy of enjoying the present, since no one knows what the future may bring and we were discussing this on our way back. As we entered the house, Gerry said he was hungry and we decided to have a late supper in the dining room. The room was softly lit by candles, the latest recording of one of our favorite records, Chuck Mangione's *The Children of Sanchez* was playing in the background and our faces had a glow of happiness. Then the nightmare started.

We heard a noise in the bedroom above us, but thought an animal might have found its way through the terrace door. Gerry told me to stay where I was and proceeded up the stairs, then across the indoor balcony, which ran along the living room wall towards the bedroom above. I went to the living room, looked up, saw him stop when the bedroom door opened and two men jumped out and wrestled him to the floor. A fight followed as he desperately tried to overcome his assailants without success. He was stabbed then, without knowing it.

Two other men rushed down to neutralize me, while another one burst through the front door. I ran back to the dining room hoping to escape through a window, but was grabbed and thrown to the floor. I was doing the best I could to fight, when I heard Gerry calling out to me, "Stop fighting and do what they want, they are too many to resist." By then he knew we did not have a chance against five strong men wearing ski masks and armed with guns and knives.

One of them grabbed my long hair and with a powerful yank sent me flying across the tile floor to the other side of the living room where they had Gerry on the floor with his hands and feet tied. And now it was my turn to be tied, with my hands behind my back. They placed us both face down on the floor, with our heads close to each other so that only one man was needed to watch us. But two of our assailants were making sure we kept our heads down and did not see what they were doing. These two men took turns questioning us. Questions we did not understand. "Where is it? Where did you hide it?" We did not know what they were looking for, but suspected they were looking for drugs. Mendocino was not far from Ukiah, a haven for marijuana growers. Was this a case of mistaken identity? The house was the largest in the entire county and might have attracted attention, but why did they think we knew something. Of the two men watching us, one was acting nice, reassuring us that everything would be all right if we told him what he wanted to know and cooperated. The other was brutal and enjoyed the fear he provoked. He pulled my arms to the breaking point till I screamed in agony, turned to Gerry and viciously kicked him where he had been wounded. While this was going on, we could hear numbers being shouted across the house. Each time a number was called out, the men would change what they were doing and would start searching a new area.

One of the thoughts I had at that time, was that history was repeating itself. Early that morning, I had read in the paper that it was the tenth anniversary of the Sharon Tate murder. Were we going to be butchered like the people who happened to be at the Tate's house that night?

Fifteen minutes had passed when they demanded my purse. After throwing my wallet on the floor, one man called a number and everything stopped. Four of the men left, leaving one behind, the cruel one. He held a gun over our heads and waited for the others to get out of the house. I was sure it was the end for us.

I remembered a Silva method technique I learned years before, for when uncertain and possibly dangerous situations were going on. I started to visualize white light surrounding us. Like a spool of white wool, I used a white ray to go over and over the two of us, using this glowing thread to go around and around, again and again. I felt the energy becoming so intense that my body started to feel very warm and all my fears stopped. A feeling of intense peace came over me. Even today, as I recall the events of that moment, I am totally astonished by the calm and peace I felt at the time. For a few minutes the man stood there with his gun pointing down towards us. But he never fired. I still believe he was prevented from killing us by forces stronger than all of us. I was given the gift of life one more time and would never forget it.

When the detective had finished questioning me, I was taken to Gerry's hospital room. He was wide awake and waiting for me. The doctor in the room understood my fear of being alone and ordered a small bed to be brought to the room, so that I could stay in the hospital overnight. I knew the following day would be hard, as the police wanted to do a reenactment of the night before.

The scene was worse than I thought. The house was surrounded by police and when I entered the living room the sight was horrifying as there was much more blood than I remembered. I felt sick and shaky. After I did my best to satisfy the police, a friend of ours showed up and told the police I had had enough. She put her arms around me, dragged me out of the house and took me back to her home where she gave me several glasses of slivovitz, very strong plum liquor, until I felt sleepy and groggy. She put me in bed and I finally collapsed and slept for the first time in forty-eight hours. I did not even know this woman well. She was mostly a friend of Gerry's, but she took charge and took care of me when I felt disconnected from the world. She was a gift from the universe to help me through a terrifying time.

When Gerry felt better, we drove to my house in Mill Valley, where we could be together but far away from the house where we both had such horrible memories. On the way, he reminded me that he had sold his house some months before to a younger man who wanted to move in later that year. The man had asked if Gerry could stay and take care of the house until the fall, when he would move in with his girlfriend and their two-year-old son. The weekend before the attack, the new owner had stopped by for a visit, supposedly to get familiar with the place. Thinking about it now made us aware that during his visit the new owner could have brought some drugs and hidden them in the garage, or someplace where Gerry would never find them

Being happy to have sold his house, Gerry never asked himself too many questions about the buyer. But he always had strange feelings about him. The house had been hard to sell because Betty Marvin, who wanted a house big enough to receive her Hollywood friends, had created a white elephant that was out of touch with reality and the average Mendocino home.

It took a long time for the police to find out what happened that night. But we read the story later in the *New York Times*. The young buyer turned out to be one of the largest drug dealers on the East Coast. The police never found any suspects, but they told us that we were attacked by an extremely well-organized criminal group with powerful connections behind it and we obviously had been targeted as the new owners of the house.

Because we were spiritually connected, two nights before the attack, we woke up at the same time, sat up in bed and both said "I had a nightmare." We had dreamed about thieves shooting him in the chest. It was difficult to believe how accurate our dreams had been, except for the fact that he was stabbed instead of shot.

Gerry stayed in Mill Valley with me for a while. Meditation and lots of conversations helped us through. But it became time for him to leave so we could start a normal life again. He bought a condominium in Marin County and left soon after.

I was so lucky to have been aware of the universal laws. I believe that by keeping my thinking positive and working on the white light during the attack, I had saved our lives. Thinking about how we can control our emotions with the help of meditation, I was happy that here I was, a few weeks after being through a life-threatening experience and feeling calm and at peace, ready to go on with my life.

At first I could not see why I had attracted such malevolent forces into my life. Not long after the event, I would learn about the laws of attraction. When the attack occurred, I had a lesson to learn. I was younger and took a lot of chances. I never thought my life would ever be connected with guns, but in fact it was and I realized I had to change some things in my life. Today, I keep away from violent movies and prefer to watch romantic ones. I concentrate more on the beauty around me and stop often to appreciate my surroundings. I choose my friends carefully and avoid aggressive people. This new perspective would not change me all at once, but it did keep me positive no matter what happened. By accepting the highs and the lows, I learned to trust my destiny even more. Sometimes I felt like soaring, while other times I felt unfulfilled, as if I had learned nothing at all. But no matter what, I knew deep down that every day in every way I was better and better.

A few months later, my relationship with Gerry changed. Traumas in a couple can take a heavy toll, as partners may react differently to their circumstances. We had to let go of each other in order to breathe better. So we went our separate ways but would always remain friends. It was a gift to have had someone I was so connected with, who had similar values and searched for the truth in the same way. I missed him for a long time.

I want to recall an event that happened to me a few months later that had to do with the laws of attraction.

As I was driving through San Rafael one day after work, I glimpsed a wallet lying in the middle of the street. Traffic was heavy and it was a difficult place to stop. But I thought of how I would feel if I had been the one losing my wallet, so I took the time to find a parking place, crossed the street and fetched the wallet.

It contained over three hundred dollars, lots of credit cards and a driver's license with the name, address and phone number of the owner. I went to the nearest phone and called him. My first words were "Relax, I found your wallet." I was surprised to hear an annoyed voice telling me he did not lose his wallet. After I insisted he should check to make sure, he returned to the phone and, profoundly disturbed and apologetic, he told me it was missing. I said "I do not live far away from you and will drop it off shortly." When I arrived to his house he insisted he wanted to give me a reward. I thanked him but I refused and went home.

One week later, on a Saturday morning, the phone rang early and an unknown voice asked me if I was Arlette Noirclerc. Upon my confirmation, the voice said "Relax, I have your wallet. It was found on a bus going to Eureka, where I am calling you from and I can put it back on another bus returning to Mill Valley, where you could pick it up." I was totally unaware I had lost my wallet and replied there must be a mistake. The lady insisted I check my purse and, sure enough, my wallet was gone. I remember shaking while I made arrangements to get my wallet back. The whole thing was like *déjà vu*, too strange to be real. But it was real, the same words were used and I had to accept the fact that the laws of attraction were extremely powerful. Since that day, I have lived my life knowing that whatever I do, good or bad, kind or unkind, words or deeds, everything could come back to me. And it always does.

Chapter Nineteen

Becoming an Entrepreneur

L ike seeds in a well-tended garden, ideas can grow from something you read in a newspaper, from a conversation with a friend, or more often from your own garden of thoughts. In the early 1980s, the dollar was at an all-time high and the franc was low. It was an excellent time to make use of my connections at Christian Dior. I could import designer fabrics from France, have my own designs made and resell the garments in my own shop.

Despite the difficult time I had with my Boston shop, I wanted to be a designer more than ever. I had to find the right location and wanted to be near Union Square, right in the center of San Francisco, where all the better shops and designers were. With the money from the sale of my home in Cohasset, Massachusetts, I was able to invest in the right location. Determination and conviction led me to a small shop on Maiden Lane, just behind Gucci. That space was vacant and reasonable in price because nobody else wanted it. It was dark and customers had to use stairs to go down to the shop level, a big deterrent to any business. This obstacle was all I needed to put my imagination in action. With a few strokes of my pencil, I redesigned the floor plan, bringing up the front part of the shop to street level and creating a few steps to go down to the back, where the office and dressing rooms were. My landlord was delighted, as I was paying for all the remodeling. With the help of a contractor's ingenuity, we were finished in four weeks.

While the remodeling was going on, I went to France to buy fabrics from Dior, Yves Saint Laurent, Chanel and a few others. I had never imported goods in large quantities before, so I hired an importer who simplified the paperwork and had my shipment delivered quickly to the shop.

Finding the right pattern-maker was easy, but finding the right workshop to create my garments was much more complicated and took more time. I finally succeeded the day I found a woman from the Philippines who had eight employees working for her. Her business was large enough to produce what I needed, but small enough to do some work by hand, giving the clothes a look of *haute couture.*

There was no doubt in my mind I had received a lot of help and guidance in setting up this new venture. Too many coincidences happened at the right time, from finding a location on Maiden Lane, meeting the right people to do my clothes, to connecting with a contractor who happened to have had a cancelation and had an opening in his schedule to be able to start my project right away. All of these "coincidences" were signs showing me the way.

I hosted a grand opening with clothes made in my new workroom, along with the gowns made in India, all of which were waiting to be unpacked after being in storage for so long. My guests were greeted with champagne and a fashion show that I prepared with great care. It was received with a lot of enthusiasm. People applauded and empty bottles were piling up. It felt wonderful.

Before long, I received invitations to do fashion shows all over San Francisco. I remember in particular a 1985 show at the World Trade Center Club attended by two hundred and fifty people. The electrical system went off and I had to choose between having music or the commentator, I could not have both. It was a huge disappointment because I had orchestrated the whole show based on a powerful piece of rock music and I had to choose the commentator. I believe that this was another lesson in acceptance and humility.

Another fashion show was to celebrate Erte's ninetieth birthday. It was done in association with a well-known gallery. The building that housed the gallery had been designed by Mies Van der Rohe and was built in a spiral like the Guggenheim in New York. It was ideal for a show. The gallery carried Erte's jewelry and the owner allowed my models to wear all the artist's beautiful pieces, to their delight and mine. It was raining heavily outside, yet the place was packed with onlookers and a few reporters. I felt on top of the world.

I spared no expense in building my new business and I started to be recognized by a few local newspapers and magazines. I hired a bright young woman to be the manager of the shop and her loyal devotion was a great support. Cheryl had an extraordinary memory for faces and names. She could remember people she had seen only once, even months before. She was the perfect business associate. I would often call on her to remind me of details about people who were important to my business.

It was hard not to become intoxicated with the recognition and the admiration my customers gave me. Some of the better-known magazines sent people to take me out to lunch. Before long, success made me forget my early beginnings and my ego got in the way. I should have remembered everything I got and be thankful for what was given to me by the universe. But I took things for granted.

I would be reminded of my ingratitude not too long after this, when I was at the height of my success. I still had many hard lessons to learn.

———

In the middle of building my business, my medical lawsuit went to trial and I lost on a technicality. The verdict was very hard to accept and the legal expenses had been high. I had to sell my jewelry to cover the costs and the unfairness of it all was hard to bear. I tried to meditate to ease the pain, but I felt betrayed and did not at first accept the verdict gracefully. It was years later that I finally understood why this had happened and why it turned out to be for the best, as it taught me one of the harshest lessons I ever had to learn.

I firmly believe today that if I had won at the time, I would not have been wise enough to know how to spend the millions of dollars involved. And I would not have had to struggle to find ways to survive and make a living. I never would have opened my businesses and never would have learned what I know today about overcoming hardship. This was a painful and gut wrenching experience which took a long time to heal as I was angry and hurt. Through it all, my only consolation was that I knew time would take care of the pain. I never stopped meditating and thought I regained my power.

In San Francisco, my business had started to take off and I was pleased to see it grow. That is, until the world of finance changed abruptly at the end of 1985 and the dollar fell sharply on the world market. All of a sudden, I found it impossible to buy goods in France because the cost became extravagant. Since the business was created on the concept of French designer fabrics, I found myself having serious difficulties.

I watched helplessly as my business turned for the worst. The day-to-day operation became a struggle and was wearing me down. What I had started with so much hope was turning into a nightmare. It was not easy to accept the idea that once more, my business was in trouble. I found myself in a repeat situation, but this time it was worse. I would be wiped out.

─────

As usual, a window opened in my life and the universe sent me help. It came in the form of the most wonderful human being I had ever met. A man named Art came into my life to teach me what real, unselfish love was. I met him in a small church in Mill Valley during one of their annual dinners. I was not going to church often, but I felt lonely at the time and needed to meet new people. Art crossed the entire dining-room full of people to be near me and start a conversation. He had first asked the minister if I was single and upon her answer he decided he wanted to know me better. His gentle and friendly manners made me accept a dinner invitation. He would become a friend and a pillar of strength when everything came crashing down.

Not long after we met, I was hospitalized for two weeks for severe chest pains. I was put in the cardiac ward and was told I was having a heart attack. Fortunately, my cardiologist kept insisting it was not a heart attack and ordered an angiogram. It was in the 1980s and it was a new procedure. After the test, I was released from the hospital and was told I did not have a heart condition. Instead, the pain came from severe esophageal spasms caused by extreme stress. My doctor gave me the choice of ending my business or risking losing my life.

How do you choose? I loved designing and supervising the creation of a new line. I lived through my fashion shows and relished the applause. I also knew that by closing the business I would lose every cent I had. There was no question in my mind, though, that I would not claim bankruptcy, as I was determined to pay every supplier who ever trusted me. Despite the threat that I would have nothing left at all, common sense told me I had to close the shop and find a new way to survive.

I had always been interested in real estate, so with friends encouraging me, I made up my mind to pursue a real estate career. I gave myself six weeks to close the business, just enough time to get my real estate license by going to school at night. I did not have any money left to pay for my apartment, so Art offered me his guest room till I could get back on my feet. I was in the worst financial condition I had ever known. But I got satisfaction in knowing that my suppliers, the bank and my landlord had been paid, leaving me with no further debts.

Art helped me face each day with hope and the certainty that I would get through this difficult time. He encouraged me to forget the past and, because of him and meditation, I was able to regain my positive attitude. This was becoming a pattern whereupon I would go through some traumatic experiences, lose my positive thoughts and then after working on them, regain my balance again.

I quickly learned real estate and worked very hard at becoming a good agent. It was the fabulous eighties, when new agents could do well if they were willing to work hard. I loved playing with figures and had learned to do income projections, so I became a specialist in investing and helped quite a few speculators. Art suggested that I stay in his house until I saved enough money to buy my own place.

After several months, my son Robin decided to come to California. It was such a joy to have him want to come to live with me. Art opened his second guest room for him and they became good friends.

In some ways, Art became like a surrogate father to Robin. With a lot of Art's patience and care, Robin started to open up and shed some of the negative baggage he had been carrying with him dating back to the divorce. He spent close to one year with us before going back to Boston. During that time, he took all kinds of jobs that did not seem to fit but he never got discouraged by the work he had to do. Art and I admired his tenacity and willpower.

Two years had gone by when I had enough money to put a deposit on a condominium. I bought it directly from the builder, before he was finished with his project. Buying from a blueprint allowed me to get it at a reasonable price.

Two years later, I resold it for much more, making my first venture in real estate very profitable and encouraging. This new endeavor showed me a way to rebuild my equity. I started to look for houses nobody wanted, bought them, moved into them, remodeled them and resold them at a profit.

For the following six years, I moved every six months, or every year or two. My family and friends were tired of updating their address books and thought I was getting unstable or flaky. But I knew my moves would pay off and they did. Each time, the house was bigger and more valuable and the profits became more and more substantial. I became an expert at picking the right house to remodel and became a speculator. I was determined to regain all the money I lost and more. I had known the bottom, I wanted to know the top. Money had never been very important in my life, but I knew how to enjoy life and all the pleasure money could buy, so I worked extremely hard to get there.

Chapter Twenty

A Very Big Mistake

During most of my adult life, I felt guided and followed what I thought was right. But there was a time I acted on impulse, when I did not feel anything at all, when life had become too much and I did not want to listen to my inner voice. It was when I thought I could deal with life on my own.

While I was still operating my shop in San Francisco and before I met Art, I went through a period of feeling sorry for myself. It was during that time that I made the biggest mistake of my life and questioned my judgment for a long time after it was all over.

Often, when I arrived in Paris for my buying trips, my brother would be waiting for me at the airport. One year, not too long after I opened my Maiden Lane shop, Roby was busy at the time of my arrival and called a friend of ours, asking him to pick me up. Guy had a lot of time on his hands. He was living alone, having lost his wife ten years before and had just recently retired. He was always looking for things to do.

Half asleep after a fifteen hour trip from San Francisco, I did not, at first, recognize our summer friend. I let out a small scream when a tall man yanked my suitcase, gave me a huge hug and kissed me on the cheek. He was ten years older. I had been a friend of both him and his wife since I was a teenager. I had not seen him for a long time and the death of his wife had left some scars on him, making him appear older than his sixty-two years.

As we were driving to my brother's apartment, we never stopped talking about the good old times when we were younger, dancing the night away with our group of friends, enjoying the warm summer nights on our favorite Oléron Island. He asked me if, after I was rested, he could come back and take me out to lunch. As it was Sunday, I could be back early enough to spend the rest of the day with my family, so I said yes.

He remembered my favorite foods were oysters and lobsters, so he took me to a restaurant specializing in oysters, any size you liked. I had never seen such a mountain of oysters on one plate. I was concentrating so much on the food that I might have eaten close to two dozen oysters before I heard what he was saying to me. He offered to take me to all my business appointments so I would not have to take taxis everywhere. He also asked if I would like to go the theater or to a fancy restaurant for dinner.

For one week, he took me everywhere and I started to warm up to this old friend who was being so nice to me. I always loved Paris at night, the lights everywhere and the life that never ends. We took long walks along the Seine and I felt quite secure with him, having known him for so long.

This business trip had turned into a pleasure trip. So, quite naturally, I asked him to visit me in San Francisco and told him I would show him California. He was eager to come and suggested he would visit in April, only three months away and take me out on my birthday, which was always a special occasion.

When he did come, we had a good time exploring the beauty of Marin County driving up and down the coast. But he had special plans in mind. One day, out of the blue, as we were looking at the beauty of the Golden Gate Bridge, he said, "When would you like to get married?"

Completely taken by surprise and more or less thinking it was a joke, I answered, "August would be fine." But he was serious and told me he would be willing to move to the States after we were married so I could go on with the career I loved.

He thought he could adapt to the American way of life, even though he could not speak English.

This was a time in my life when I felt it would be nice to have someone taking care of me for a change. Guy had shown he cared and respected my sense of independence. He was very attentive to my needs and was so nice that it was easy to think marrying him was a good idea. Also, we had known each other for so long that we assumed we knew each other well. So I said "yes" and we decided August would be a good month for a wedding. We could get married on the island of Oléron with all our friends and family. We called our respective families to tell them the news; they were surprised but congratulated us warmly.

In France, there is a civil ceremony before you can be married in a church. In our case, things got a little complicated when we found out my American divorce from Andrew had never been registered in France and I could not get married to Guy without breaking the law. Fortunately, his sister was the mayor of a small community and she pulled a few strings in order to be able to marry us. From there, we drove to Oléron for our religious wedding and then a party thrown by my sister and brother, in the garden of our family house. The tables were under the trees, which had been adorned with lights and we danced late into the night.

I never knew what happened to the sweet man I married. The day after our wedding, he changed into a different man. I thought I had clearly explained how independent I was, but Guy never heard me or did not want to hear what I had to say. In his mind, we were a couple and had to do everything together, including going to the market, going to see friends, choosing a piece of clothing or going to the beach. He did not leave me alone for one minute. It all started during our honeymoon, which we spent sailing on his boat.

It went on for the following two weeks in Paris, before flying out to the States. After a while, I told him we had a problem that we needed to discuss, but he refused to talk about it. When he became totally silent I realized this was serious. I was not sure about taking him back with me to the States, but I convinced myself things could change and that he could, once more, become the sweet man I had married. I was determined to make my marriage work.

Things became even worse in San Francisco, as he felt lost and turned his frustration on me. He sulked wordlessly for days at a time. I had a hard time dealing with the silence and I finally became very sick. After only two months of married life, the doctor told me that all my symptoms were psychological and were the result of a deep traumatic shock to my system. I went home and asked Guy to go back to France, as we could not live together any more.

The worst for me was that I had to face my two sons and explain to them I was going to get a divorce after only three months of marriage. Young people are amazing and I could not believe the response I got from them. Philip was the first to hear the news and said, "Gee, Mom, it's nice to know that at your age you can make such a blunder."

Robin was quite direct. He said, "Mom, I never felt at ease with him and I am glad you made that decision."

After Guy left, I went back to my business, plunging heartily into designing to forget the last few months. Thinking back, I believe Guy never realized how independent I was. He refused to see the businesswoman in me and might have been threatened by my ideas and imagination. I believe he thought my independence was something else, not what it was: a long life I built on my own, making lots of decisions by myself and without anybody's approval or support. I blamed myself for getting involved in a situation like this and for a while questioned my ability to make the right decisions.

Since the universe never let me down, I finally realized that I had gotten off the path I was on before. After the disaster of my medical lawsuit, I faced the fact that I was not meditating regularly anymore and started to complain often. I had been ungrateful and was reminded of it. The moment I became conscious of what was going on, I decided to change my attitude, work on positive thinking and with the help of the universe I started to rebuild my life. Within weeks I had regained my faith and with it came back my *joie de vivre*.

Chapter Twenty-One

The Earthquake

My California real estate venture was going well. After six years, I had learned to pick winners. I took calculated risks and always saw in my mind what I could do to change the look of "dog houses," as the realtors called them and make these houses attractive. But I was getting tired of constantly moving and started to think it was time to stop doing this. The thought of settling down for a while was very appealing to me.

When I looked at what would be my last speculation, I did not have to ask myself why this house had not sold at the height of the real estate boom. It had dark paneling, smelly brown shag carpeting and holes in the doors and walls, among other problems. The kitchen and baths were a disaster. To top it all, the basement had dog droppings that had never been cleaned and the house had termite damage. It had been rented to a couple who had an attack dog and apparently grew marijuana in the basement and attic.

It was an enormous undertaking. But I knew I could turn this house around and make a wonderful house to live in, or sell it at a great profit. The owners were happy to receive an offer and accepted a very low price.

It took me six months to redo it, but the end result was quite astounding. One of its biggest assets had always been a fabulous view from the terrace overlooking the valley. After I was through redecorating, the finished product was very different from the shabby house I had purchased and I was proud to live in it.

About one year after I purchased the house, my older son Philip was transferred by his brokerage firm to California and he decided to come and live with me. It was a pleasure to know he would be staying with me. I could not have been happier.

My friend Art visited every day and was always ready to add some finishing touches on the house. He was handy with woodworking and liked to help me with my redecorating projects. Art was a widower and we were the greatest friends. We knew we could never be more. We were too different in our tastes and lifestyles and it seemed our differences made it impossible for us to pursue our relationship further. He would remarry eventually and we kept in touch for a while as he was always in my thoughts as one of my close friends.

One day, Philip and I were having dinner when we heard a terrific noise like a bomb explosion. Then the earth shook. I had been through several small earthquakes before, but this one was different. The shocks were stronger and the ground rolled like a roller coaster. We had just enough time to rush under an entryway. I grabbed two bike helmets and handed one to Philip. He looked outside and observed a woman walking right under the power lines, apparently too traumatized to be logical. He ran out, took her by the arm and forced her away from the electric poles, which were starting to collapse along the road. He told her to stay under our entryway until the earth stopped moving.

I looked at the ceiling and saw the house move from right to left and back again. After three or four minutes everything stopped. It was frightening, but we were all right.

We were thrilled to see that the house was still standing and undamaged. Built at the top of a hill, it could have been shaken loose from its foundation and made its way down the slope. But it survived the earthquake with flying colors. The noise we had heard when the earthquake started was an electric junction box, which blew up close to the house.

I felt very grateful we had not been harmed, but was worried when Philip left for San Francisco. He drove down to the city from

Mill Valley, where we were, to see if he could help earthquake victims. When he came back, he described how badly the water front had been damaged.

The area in question was called the Marina, a section of San Francisco that was entirely built on a land-fill. The ground was too soft to handle an earthquake of this magnitude. Entire blocks were cordoned off. Quite a few houses were leveled to the ground. The police were everywhere and people were walking or standing helplessly, waiting to be told what to do. Some people wanted to go back to their houses to evaluate the damage but were forbidden to do so, as their homes might collapse at any moment. The police did not want any help and just wanted people to leave the area.

It was heartbreaking to hear the details of this huge catastrophic event. As I heard later from friends who lived in the Marina, the devastation had affected many people and it would take years before the area would be back to normal. One friend was taking a bath when the quake happened. The shock was so violent that she found herself in a near-empty bathtub.

The news on television kept us informed about the fate of the people who had been trapped on the collapsed Oakland Bay Bridge and on the search for survivors. Every day we had to deal with new after-shocks. For two weeks my nerves were on edge. When a policeman stopped me for making the wrong turn, I started to cry. He was so surprised by my reaction that he offered to follow me home, to make sure I was all right. I thanked him and declined his offer, then was shocked that he still gave me a ticket. Over the ten years I was in California I found the police very cold, terribly strict and always ready to give you a ticket. They were very different from the police in other states.

Because of the earthquake I started to think California was not such a safe place to live. The idea of moving back east was planted in my mind.

―∞∞∞―

One day, Philip came home from work all excited. There was a new agent at his firm and he told me how beautiful this young woman was. As he was talking, I understood right away this girl was special to him and I told him I would love to meet her. Very shortly after that I met Carey, without knowing then, that she would become my daughter-in-law. When Philip was asked by his superior to transfer to France, he told me he would ask Carey to go to Paris with him. They stayed there for two years, came back to the States and got married a couple of years later.

After Philip left California, I felt the absence of my two sons more than ever. This, coupled with the strong emotions I had about the earthquake, reinforced my dream of going back east. The traumas of my divorce in Boston did not exist anymore. Ten years had gone by and many things had changed, including my relationship with Andrew. We had become friends again and were talking to each other.

Weighing the pros and cons of leaving California, I became aware that the only thing I would miss would be my friendship with Art. My mind was made up.

⬥

One day, as I was standing at the edge of the Sausalito marine area, I looked at the incredible sight of San Francisco Bay. The Golden Gate Bridge on my left stretched across the bay. In the mid-afternoon, shadows cast over the water were moving along with the current. It was like a well-orchestrated ballet. The beauty of it was too much to describe.

How could I possibly want to leave this place? The first day I saw the grandiose bridge I thought my destiny had brought me home. But I found out home was with the people I loved surrounding me. San Francisco was not the paradise I thought I had found.

I was overwhelmed by a burst of silent rage. What did I have to learn to achieve peace? Years of meditation had given me some sort of tranquility, but not yet happiness and peace. The certainty I had about being guided was strong. I could not doubt that feeling. My life had been a continuous adaptation to change and the only two constants were the love I had for my children and my spiritual beliefs. I had to accept the fact that the universe, or stronger forces than I, knew the reason for my gypsy life.

I mentally prepared to go back east, closer to my children. It took two years after the earthquake for me to put my house on the market, sell it, find the right one back east and close my real estate business.

I went back to New England to search for a multifamily house near the ocean that could bring me enough income until I could figure out what to do to provide for my everyday living expenses. After a few trips, I zeroed in on Newport, Rhode Island. It was the closest town to Boston I could find where there were very large houses converted into apartments, perfect for me. ,

One thing led to another and before long, I became a landlord to five tenants. I was the proud owner of a seven-thousand-square-foot house that had been made into six apartments. I called it "My Castle."

The move from California was easy, but I lost a few things that meant a lot to me, including a box containing my favorite books. I was not happy to know that somebody else was enjoying quite a few dedicated treasures that never made it back east. This was one of the prices to pay for my many moves.

I arrived in my new town without knowing a soul but determined to make it work. Philip and Carey had moved to Connecticut after their wedding; Robin followed them shortly after that. I was looking forward to having all of us together often, as they were so close to Newport. I also was happy about the hour-and-a-half drive to Boston, which would allow me to see my old friends.

Chapter Twenty-Two

The Universe

Throughout this recollection of my life journey, I have talked about the universe often. It is time for me to explain what the word universe means to me.

My father was a member of the Reformed Church and my mother descended from a line of Huguenots, who survived the religious wars in a predominantly Roman Catholic country. Her family was proud of the fact that one of our ancestors was the last martyr burned alive during those terrible wars. History books disagree and claim he was hanged instead, in a small village in 1746. But my mother's family never changed their version of a woman approaching him with a torch and setting fire to his beard, while a crowd watched and cheered in a public square.

His name was Mathieu Desubas and he is honored in the now famous *Musee du Desert* in southern France. The museum recalls the lives of the Huguenots after the revocation of the *Edit de Nantes* signed by Louis XIV in 1685. The edict revoked the right of the Huguenots to practice their faith. It was considered one of Louis XIV's worst mistakes, as it started the war of religions all over again. The museum displays books and testimonials by the Huguenots during their struggle against the King for their religious freedom. They were persecuted in their mountain bastion called *Les Cevennes*, a rugged part of France, only accessible by winding through the chain of mountains on narrow roads. When my mother and I drove through that part of southern France, I recalled thinking my ancestors must have been just like the mountains surrounding us, rough, strong, hard on themselves and also stubborn. They had to have been, in order to survive and keep their faith.

While growing up I respected and embraced my parents' beliefs. In many ways, I still do, but my life experiences led me to believe there was more to life's mysteries than what I learned from my parents. As a young child I drove my mother crazy asking her why things happened the way they did. When I was ten years old, I nearly was expelled from a Roman Catholic school after students complained I was trying to convert them to my religion. When the principal gave me a choice of stopping my recruiting or facing the consequences, I remember throwing this phrase at her: "Why? There are so many of you and only one of me."

In my teens, I read a book called *Human Destiny*, which reconciled God and science. It was written by Le Comte Du Nouy and is still in print today, more than sixty years later. It was meaningful to me because it showed me there are many different ways to look at religions and people have a natural desire to search for the truth and share their ideas with others.

When I moved to the United States, I was not affiliated with any particular religion, but I remained interested in spirituality. I was lucky enough to attract the people I needed along the way to lead me to the right books and the right seminars. I also had the privilege of meeting insightful people who influenced my thinking and helped me through the maze of ideas and thoughts in the literature.

I read books about the beliefs of Buddhists, American Indians, Islamic people, Jewish people and, of course, Christians. I also attended many seminars about the Silva Method, which had a great impact on me.

One thing struck me. Faith was the common denominator. Some had faith in God or gods and some had faith in things or beliefs. Some believed in Heaven and some in reincarnation. Most believed in a power stronger than themselves.

I chose a philosophy of faith in one's self, given to us by a superior force. The ability to create miracles depends on the amount of faith in the power you have. To me, the universe gave us the power to create the life we want to lead. I believe that if we don't have faith in ourselves, we lose our power. When we are under stress or pain, we create alpha waves so strong that they put us into a meditative state. So it is when I am under tremendous stress or pain that I have enough faith to create miracles.

Why not believe we can create miracles? I have experienced it in my own life and seen that we have the ability to do so, provided we are willing to do the work and have enough faith in the process. The Bible says God created man in His image. So it is not difficult to see we have the ability to help ourselves and create our own miracles.

In order to become aware of this simple truth, we have to follow the laws of the universe. Some of these laws we learn from our parents, but there are so many more. The first one I discovered is faith. I found it helpful that each time I encountered difficulties, I had the absolute certitude I would be all right no matter what happened. Even if my problems were still there, the faith in my beliefs made my pains easier to bear and calmed my anxieties.

This simple way of going through life made all the difference to me. If I needed clarity in something, all I had to do was concentrate and visualize a solution and before long I would find myself in a bookstore facing the right book, or a friend would suggest the right answer. Once my direction was set, all I needed was the desire and the willingness to do the work necessary to succeed. *Awareness of the power to create is key.*

If faith and awareness are key, then gratitude is the magnifier. I have been thankful for all the gifts I received and it seems to me that the more grateful I was, the more rewards I got.

Coincidences do not happen in my life. I believe my positive attitude attracts what I need to have and to know. The more strongly positive I am, the more "coincidences" happen. It's like a magnet. People attract what they think about. Of course, it is not always easy, but with time and patience I have learned to concentrate on the good things and push away destructive thoughts.

This is what I learned following the laws of the universe. Why do I call it the universe? Nature and the world taught me much more than what I learned in Sunday school. I do not like the idea that creating miracles for ourselves makes us God-like. But it is because we were created with such power that, with enough faith, we can accomplish what seems to be the impossible.

Some powerful forces created universal laws. To me, it does not matter who, or why. But I know they exist to help us find the right answers. I meditate and pray to God, but I feel we were given the power to heal ourselves and give God a rest. So I use my awareness to read through the details of my life and improve myself along the way. But I acknowledge that I still have a great deal to learn.

As I went through many ups and downs, I found out that what I thought were big problems or disappointments turned out for the best and gave me the benefit of learning what I was supposed to learn. Awareness is like a wonderful gift given to all who want to improve their journey, with peace of mind and tranquility. At the end of this book, I will give a list of the universal laws that changed my life.

Chapter Twenty-Three

The Land of Tides

I moved to Newport in the summer of 1990. It was an exciting town and I felt happy and light, like the air in the trees. On the day of closing on a new house, I left the attorney's office with my heart pounding. I could not wait to drive down Rhode Island Avenue and go around the block, one more time, to admire the beauty of my new home.

The lot was large and covered a whole block. In the center was a two-hundred-year old oak tree spreading its branches over part of the 7,000 square foot house.

The structure was white and stood like a miniature castle. Its tower had a huge stained-glass window that filtered color over the staircase and the front door was framed by columns. Like many large houses in Newport, there was a small carriage house in the back of the property. The property was built by a banker in the 1880s and remained in the same family until 1960, when it was sold and made into separate apartments.

As I drove around to look at my new place, I thought about how my hard work and determination had paid off and I let myself admire the place. Owning this small estate was the result of many real estate transactions in California. I felt proud and thankful to have been given this new beautiful home.

But I felt a bit frustrated that I could not move in right away. There was a mix-up with the tenants who occupied the apartment I wanted and they would not be moving out for another month. I also had to wait for my furniture to arrive. My plan was to move into the main apartment and keep the tenants in the other five apartments for income.

My place was the largest with a living room that was forty-five feet in length, with a six-foot hearth and ten-foot ceilings. I dreamed of parties and family reunions, imagining I would stay there forever to receive the grandchildren I wanted to have someday. I knew it was a challenge, but I also knew my imagination would help.

I first had to introduce myself to the tenants, who were not happy to have a new landlord. People dread changes and I was quite aware it would take time before they warmed up to me. I reassured them, smiled a lot and hoped for the best. Three weeks later my furniture arrived from California, one week afterwards, the apartment became available and I moved in.

I had just finished putting my furniture into place when Hurricane Bob decided to make an appearance in Newport. It was 1990 and it was the first time I found myself in a hurricane. After having been through an earthquake in San Francisco and now facing a hurricane, I wondered what lesson I had to learn from all this. One of my friends was visiting from France and thought she was not lucky to have picked that particular time to come and visit me. But she realized there was nothing she could do and felt this was going to be a new adventure.

Being in an old house made of stone helped us not to be so afraid. The wind made an incredible noise outside. Then it stopped. I remember that eerie feeling when the silence took place. It became overwhelming and the air felt so light we felt intoxicated. I knew this was the eye of the hurricane, having read about them and I braced myself for the second part of the storm. It came shortly after and, since it was the second time around, we felt quite relaxed about it. Fortunately, the damage from the storm was mostly structural and no life was lost. But lots of trees were down and the town looked like a skeleton.

My property survived well, but one of my old oak trees snapped like a matchstick and blocked the street for five days, forcing cars to go around the block. It also knocked down the power lines, plunging the entire block in darkness for an entire week. I learned the power of patience, barbecues and candles. Cleaning up the yard and cutting broken limbs and trees took about two weeks, but life went back to normal and, soon after, the noise from chainsaws faded away.

Newport was known to have a cyclical business pattern, with April through October being the busy months and the rest of the year being very quiet. I realized opening a shop there would make a lot of sense, so I spent the winter planning every detail and looking for a vacant space to open in the spring. It would be different from any of the shops I had before, but I was ready to make a go at it.

I found the perfect spot on the famous Thames Street, near the waterfront and rented it for one year with a renewable lease for three. This way I could test the waters without getting burned, in case my venture did not work. I decided not to design anymore but to buy typical summer-resort clothing, which would be easy to sell in this town. My new place was small but needed no decorating, as it had been a clothing store before. Since I had put most of my assets in the house, I borrowed some capital from a bank, putting my house as collateral. This did not scare me, as I had plenty of experience buying and running a retail business. Opening the shop in April at the beginning of the summer season would lower the risk of failing and losing the small amount of capital I invested. I called my new venture: *Belle de Jour.*

The first year was a big success and made me forget my loss in California. Sure, it was not the excitement of being a designer, but my tiny shop was making a profit and allowed me to hire two part-time employees. I ran the shop and, at home, I was an apartment manager. There was little time for the beach and parties but I was grateful for a rewarding life. I was able to receive my children and their friends as often as they wanted. Newport was a great attraction to all of them, especially when I went to France for a few weeks at a time and left them the run of the house.

Through the shop, I met two very special women who played

an important part of my life. They came in as customers and left as friends. Nicole became a friend who always volunteered ahead of everybody else to help me. Gillian became a spiritual mentor who always knew what to say when I faced her with my latest problem. She also had a fantastic sense of humor, which went well with my belief that laughter was an important part of life and relieved the pressure of taking things too seriously. Both my friends were married and were living examples of great relationships.

As much as I enjoyed the summers in Newport, I dreaded the winters. The streets were empty and there was nothing to do. The tourists were gone and half the residents returned to their winter homes elsewhere. The Newport music and jazz festivals were over until the next summer. So I filled up my time by taking long drives along the shore, admiring mansions of a long-gone era.

Most of these gigantic places were built by moguls of the nineteenth century and were a display of wealth and extravagance. Each new one was designed to be bigger or more ornate than the last one. One egocentric owner built an indoor polo arena on the ground floor of his mansion. It had a separate entrance for the horses far from where the lady of the house was entertaining her friends in the upstairs quarters. There was a frenzy to compete with the Vanderbilt and their *Breakers Estate* or their *Marble House*. A few, like the Astor, turned up their nose at this new generation of wealth and power and remained away from the splendors of the Vanderbilt parties.

I had fun showing these palaces of yesteryear to visiting friends and took the time to discover new places and enjoy the treasures of Newport's past. In a way, seeing the folly of yesterday's made me appreciate better the reality of today and its quiet moments.

One of my winter excitements was my trip to France every February, when I closed the shop for one month. I would stay in Paris with my family or friends and would do some buying for the shop.

During one of my visits to Paris, I got reacquainted with an old friend of the family, the uncle of my god child. Olivier had just gotten a divorce and knew what he wanted in life. Once he made up his mind about something, he would do anything in his power to get it. He decided he wanted to marry me and was determined to do so. It was hard to resist his charm, his humongous bouquets of flowers, gifts, trips and all the trappings money can buy. I especially appreciated these gifts after working so hard in Newport. This was not going to be an easy courtship across the Atlantic Ocean, but Olivier was sure he could make it work despite the geography. So we started a long-distance relationship in which I would go to Paris every month for one week and stay in Newport the rest of the time to run my business.

During that first year, I spent the whole month of August in his thirteenth century castle in central France. This was an extraordinary place. It had the only running moat among castles that old. It had been faithfully restored, was registered as an historical place by the government and was opened to the public once a week.

One morning, I had forgotten there were visitors coming and I left the private apartments to get my early cup of coffee, running down the stairs with a robe on. To my dismay, I found myself facing a crowd of about fifteen people at the bottom of the stairs looking up at me in disbelief. Dignity lost, I thought the only way out was to smile, say "Bienvenue," and run back upstairs. The visitors must have been quite amused by my embarrassment.

After one year of commuting between France and the United States, Olivier insisted I move back to France so we could learn more about each other under normal circumstances and consider getting married. It was a difficult decision to make, as I knew I had to close my shop and move to Paris if I wanted to marry Olivier. Most of the pressure came from my French family, who could not understand why I would not say "yes" faster.

I have always believed you have to follow your heart and your instincts. But I was not sure about marrying Olivier yet, so I decided to move forward without taking a full plunge. I would move to Paris, keep my house, put a manager in charge of the apartments and close the shop. All these changes were hard to do, but Olivier always had an answer for everything. So I closed the shop in the winter of 1993 and moved to an apartment in Paris close to Olivier's chic *seventh arrondissement* home in the city.

At first, things went beautifully. Olivier was very attentive and had my son Robin over for a visit, hoping he would stay in Paris so I could have one of my children on the same continent. He even offered to buy Robin a business of his choice, but even though Robin appreciated the offer, he flew back to the US. After he left I started to see some subtle changes in Olivier.

He would get terribly upset for no reason at all and had extreme mood swings. His housekeeper made me aware of the fact that she was finding empty bottles of liquor all over the apartment and was concerned for his welfare. Before I moved to Paris, we were together only for one week at a time and he never showed any difficulty controlling his liquor. But after I moved to Paris and saw him drink constantly, I started to ask myself questions about his drinking habits. He often had bursts of rage and would scream at me for no reason that I could see. After the conversation with the housekeeper, I could no longer ignore the problem. Olivier was an alcoholic and I knew it would only get worse. I also knew I had to leave before I got badly hurt, mentally or physically.

It had been four months since I had left Newport. My fairy tale was over and it was time to get back to reality again. I had known peaks of splendor and now faced lows of despair, but there was some comfort in knowing that leaving Olivier was the right thing to do. Too many friends had told me horror stories about men who drink too much and I was not about to marry such a person.

As I had closed my business and came back with my dreams up in smoke, I had a hard time remaining in the same town that Olivier visited and adored. I knew I would see him everywhere. He was a charmer and we had such a good time when he was sober that I knew I would miss him even more if I stayed in

Newport. At first I did not know what to do. But slowly, one at a time, ideas started to form in my mind and I decided to rent my apartment in Newport and move to Boston to try real estate again.

In Boston, however, I did not do well and my finances were depleting quickly. There was too much competition in real estate and it would take months or years before I could make a living at it. So I turned back to the one thing I felt I could be successful at. I opened another *Belle de Jour* in the Boston area.

After looking for the right place, I settled for an attractive window front property on a cobbled street in Winchester, a most charming New England town. It would turn out to be a small heaven, full of the best-intentioned people. They took me under their wing, helped me start the business and carried me through the next major problem waiting for me. The universe was teaching me many lessons and I was a slow learner.

Chapter Twenty-Four

Learning to Live with Cancer

Discovering I had cancer had not been on my agenda and did not fit into my theory that good mental health equals good physical health. The subject had not been easy to address in words, but I became quite aware that by avoiding talking about this part of my life, I cheated others of one of my greatest leaps of faith. My experiences in 1996 gave me an incredible chance to meet some fabulous people and taught me that the universal laws that I had been practicing did not stop bad things from happening. Rather, they helped you through them.

On April 8th, my birthday, I found myself in an operating room at Beth Israel, surrounded by a terrific team of women who were going to take a small part of me away. Nature's most feminine enhancement was going to become my new nightmare. When discovered in time, breast cancer is not so bad these days, as 6 out of 10 women will experience, but the stigma and emotional disturbance associated with the disease, are still very much present.

Lying on the hospital table, I wondered what had gotten me there. I always believed the body is a barometer telling us how well we are doing. It acts sometimes to slow us down, or makes us aware something is not quite right in our lives. Our health, good or bad, is often governed by heredity, but I believe other things added to my illness, like stress and unresolved resentments. A mental cancer became, in the end, a physical one.

Images of the past year in Boston now appeared on a screen inside my head. When I came back to the city, after the fiasco of my breakup with Olivier in France, I was carrying quite a bit of resentment. The whole affair had started with so much hope and it ended so quickly that I never had time to accept it with grace. Under the circumstances, it became difficult to make a new start. My resentments acted like a magnet and attracted more and more problems.

It started with my going back to real estate, which ended up in disaster. Then my ex-husband Andrew remarried. It was good for him, but hard for me, as I never stopped caring for him. And at the same time, my dear friend Art remarried also. I knew his marriage would change our friendship forever, as most women cannot accept female friends in their husbands' lives. And the final blow came when my sister decided to split the ocean-side property she received from our parents and sell half of it to my brother. I had always dreamed of sharing some part of it one day, but they sealed the deal before telling me about it, making it too late for me to have any say in it.

I was living in a very dark apartment in a Boston suburb and hated it. I loved sunshine and seemed to do much better in sunny places. There were a few times in the past when I felt sorry for myself, but I had never before experienced this much despair for so long. I was overwhelmed.

Neither meditation, nor the blue Boston sky, nor friends could help me. I let my own destructive forces lead me to self-pity and eventually into depression. I stopped the normal flow of positive energies that kept me healthy and chose the path that lead me to an operating table. Negativity had regained power over me, taking away my healing powers.

It was time to change what was happening. As I lay there reviewing my difficulties and searching for their purpose, the answer came to me again. I realized I had just been given a gift.

The blessing was right here, right now. By recalling the past,

I was becoming aware of what I had done to myself. It was my thoughts and my negativity that were the cause of my own hardships and cancer.

In the minutes following my awareness, I made a pact that I was going to change my mental attitude and work on appreciating the great things that I had, instead of concentrating on the bad.

The moment I shifted my thinking, everything improved. While still waiting to be operated on, I heard soft music in the background, saw smiley faces around and the nicest nurse leaned over me and said," I have a wonderful cocktail for you." Within minutes, I was flying with the angels.

Even the radiation treatments turned out to be much better than I expected. Going to the hospital in the morning allowed me to open my shop in the afternoon. Well-wishers gave me more business than I expected. When I shifted my negative energies to allow the flow of life to return again, my cancer became nothing more than just another small stone on the road.

Six months later, when I had to face another operation for a rotator cuff in my shoulder, I kept the right attitude. The doctors told me my arm would be painful for at least six months and I would need a lot of care and exercise to get my movement back.

Never before had I met so many people offering to help, people who took me to the hospital and did my shopping. Gwenda, whom I hardly knew, often took me for treatments to the hospital. Judith spent time in the shop when my arm was too painful. My dear friend Fran came every Sunday to wash my hair, as I could not use my arm. Many others showed up with smiles on their faces, including my ex-husband Andrew, who never refused to help when it was needed.

I tried to work with my arm in a sling but found it too painful. Having no manager and only novice part-time help, I decided one more time to close my shop. I was getting good at doing this. It had only been thirteen months since I had opened this location which could have been a very good venture, but the choice was not mine anymore because of my health problems.

I wrote a letter to all my customers, explaining what was happening and, within days, the word got out. In two weeks, I had sold just about everything in the shop, including all the furniture and fixtures. A friend who came to help me remove the last items could not believe we did not have enough to fill her station wagon. It was amazing and the most rewarding thing was that I did not have to reduce the price of my stock much to sell it all. The universe did the work.

These two difficult passages in my life would be a reminder that negativity attracts pain. I believe that by doing our best, we can often change the outcome of a traumatic experience. Of course, I cannot explain why so many wonderful, positive people go through very hard times. Sometimes the tragic events are impossible to understand, but I do believe that each one of us has to learn a different lesson, very much our own and each lesson is necessary for the benefit of our soul.

Now, when difficulties start appearing on the horizon, I always try to shift my energies to better thoughts. If I cannot think clearly, I will meditate. Or I might jump into a bubble bath and let the warm water sooth my nerves and body. Or I'll reach for that delicious chocolate bar while listening to my favorite music.

Some of my evening wear that was made in India

VICTORIA

ARLETTE
NOIRCLERC

VICTORIA

CHARMEUSE SILK

CREPE DE CHINE

My bestseller

Turning fifty

My home in Newport

Olivier's 15th century castle

Part Four

Chapter Twenty-Five

Moving to Florida

"Are you sure you want to move to Florida?" asked Nicole in a concerned voice.

"It's not as bad as you think," was the answer she got from me. I was aware my New England friends did not think moving to Florida was a good idea. To them, it was a place where people do nothing but play golf all day or bask in the sun.

I did not want to go into detail. How could I explain how tough these last two years had been in Boston? Two major operations had taken their toll. My doctors recommended sunshine and I was tired of the snow. My house in Newport had been on the market for almost two years without anybody showing interest in it. Florida at that time was very economical and made sense to me as I was once again without an income. I figured I could always try it as I was not afraid of new surroundings.

I was living in the Boston suburb of Arlington and moved on April 1st. 1997, during a snow storm. The snow was falling so heavily that the movers offered to carry me to my car. I decided to put my furniture in storage for a while and do some traveling to visit family and friends. I would remain in the area till I was sure that the Florida sunshine was the answer to what I was looking for.

A couple of months before leaving Arlington, I had asked my friend Gillian to take a trip with me to explore Florida's west coast and decide whether it was a good move or not. It turned out to be hectic, as I was under medication for the shoulder operation I had six weeks before and we often had to rush back to the hotel because I was not feeling well, or too tired to go on. But Gillian had a wonderful disposition and she never complained. She was an amazing person. She got up at five o'clock every morning to walk. Whether it was on the beach, a winding path or a busy street, she loved to see the sunrise.

Throughout the years I found out that one of her strengths was the ability to never get mad. On the rare occasions she got upset, she would retreat to meditate or read a book and would reappear smiling and happy. I have always felt privileged she was my friend and continue to learn a lot from her. I consider her a spiritual friend and appreciate that she is always there for me. She has been a special gift the universe gave me.

When we arrived in Florida the weather was perfect. We landed in Fort Myers and rented a car for our trip. Our first stop was Naples. It was lunchtime, so we looked for a place to eat among the numerous restaurants lining Main Street. Having satisfied our hunger, we started to stroll downtown in a leisurely manner.

Too many shops displayed expensive items and too many people rushed from one shop to the other to buy the latest faddish item they could find. As the days went by and we explored more, we started to feel uneasy. Everything was perfect, too perfect and too clean. You felt women had their hair done every day. Very few children ran around. Naples was a playground for older, wealthy people who were catered to by working people living out of town. We left, deciding the town was artificial and resembled a theater set.

We drove up the coast until we reached Sarasota. The moment we got there, both of us had a very good feeling about the town. Sarasota was spread out and divided into neighborhoods having their own personality and character. It was a working town with many businesses, which attracted all kinds of people from all over.

Sarasota also was well-known for its artist colony. We found out there were enough ballet, music and theater companies to make New York jealous. Culture made it a vibrant city full of life. It also had some of the most beautiful beaches in the world. We visited my old friends, Tom and Terry, who took us all over the place and never stopped telling us how happy they were to have chosen this part of the world for their retirement.

After four days in Sarasota, we decided we did not have to explore anything else. I was going to move to Florida and this town was my choice. We went back to Boston, satisfied with our expedition.

During the spring and the summer, I took advantage of the fact that I was jobless and effectively homeless, since my Newport house was fully rented. It was an opportunity to visit some friends and spend time in France. I returned for four months to my favorite island of Oléron on the southwest coast of France.

While I was enjoying my vacation, I got the wonderful news that my house had sold. After more than two years, someone finally was willing to buy it, make the badly-needed costly repairs and essentially bail me out. The timing was perfect, as I now could make some solid plans to move to Sarasota. I flew back home and prepared for my next move.

It was the first time I would be driving such a long way, so I decided to take the auto train south, from Washington to Orlando, Florida. It seemed like a good idea at the time and I thought I would have a peaceful night and arrive in Sarasota fresh and rested.

But it was anything but restful. The train broke down twice for a short time, then finally broke down for the day. We were in a no man's land, with no structure in sight, somewhere in Georgia. We stayed on the tracks for two hours before the electricity shut down. It was ninety-five degrees outside and we had no more air conditioning. Inside the train, the temperature rose quickly to 100 degrees and people were starting to be very upset and lose their tempers. With the lack of electricity, the toilets stopped working and started to smell.

In the middle of all this, we heard the news that Princess Diana had just died. There was some crying from among the passengers, but I did not know if it was because of the news or because of our circumstances. The atmosphere on that train was heavy. We had no choice but to wait for the rescue team.

It took about six hours before mechanics were able to fix the train so we could go on to our final destination. When we finally arrived in Orlando, I promised myself I would never again set foot on the auto train. Since then, I have driven up and down the coast many times with ease and no problem. And when I did not need my car up north, flying took only three hours.

When I arrived in Sarasota, I easily found the motel Gillian and I stayed in before, during our exploring tour. It was going to be my home until I found an apartment for rent, as I wanted to get to know the area before buying a house. Beside the bad train experience, I felt lucky to have arrived safe and sound. The familiar look of the motel reassured me and I knew I was not alone. Things were going to be just fine.

Chapter Twenty-Six

Orange Juice and Sunshine

The motel was deserted. Not a sound was heard. It was quite a change from February, when Gillian and I spent four days there. At the time, the motel was full of regular customers, mostly Canadians, escaping their long winter season. We had felt a little lost among a crowd of people searching for orange juice and sunshine. But in September, the owners were so happy to have a customer braving the heat and the humidity that they never stopped asking me if I needed anything.

My objective was to rent an apartment for six months while looking for a house to buy. I started to drive around town to get a feel for the different locations. I covered a lot of ground and eventually found an unfurnished apartment in an appealing complex with tennis courts and a swimming pool. One great factor was the fact that I could rent the apartment for a short period of time.

Right after signing the lease, I called my movers in Boston to let them know they could start their long way down to Sarasota. I was told it would take two weeks. So I decided to leave the motel and do some camping of my own, inside my new place. I bought the basics, an air mattress, folding chair, cooking utensils, sheets and towels and rented a television for two weeks. I was pleased with the result and moved in as soon as I could, anxious to leave the motel. It had been a good stopover, but had been expensive and did not feel like home.

When my movers arrived, I was glad to see my favorite antique pieces and artwork again after so long. Too many times during my numerous moves, things had been broken or lost. So I rushed to unpack my favorites and was relieved to see a Pre-Columbian collection that I gathered over the years, safe and in good condition.

I could not have stood the idea of breaking some pieces dating back to 500 BC on my watch. Or that my good luck piece, a carved wooden plaque covered in gold from the mid-seventeenth century, would get damaged. It came from the palace of Versailles, when reconstruction occurred in the 1960s and parts of the doors and walls were sold to antique dealers. This unique piece brought back memories of my childhood growing up and running around the gardens of the palace. It gave me a sense of being home.

Similarly, a few pieces of furniture contributed to my wellbeing. My mother's desk, or bedroom chest, brought me peace and reassurance during my numerous moves, when loneliness was looming at the door. I was never very much attached to things in general, but certain pieces of furniture reminded me of my mother or of my father at a time when I felt protected and never had to fend for myself.

In Sarasota, I did not waste any time and immediately looked for a job. I heard of a special shop on Saint Armand Circle selling high-end women's clothing. At the time, Saint Armand Circle was the undisputed best shopping area in Sarasota and it attracted people from all over the world. I thought I might enjoy working there for a while and learn more about the area's clientele. I walked into the most sophisticated shop and was hired immediately.

I had never worked for anybody in the U.S. before and presumed it might be difficult for me to do so now. Fashion had been my life for a long time and I knew so much about it that I was afraid I might know more than the owner of the shop. But I was determined to try something new and accepted an associate position, a glorified title for a sales clerk.

I started working right away and, for a few months,

I succeeded in doing so. But as the weeks and months went by, it became more and more difficult to stay and work in an environment I considered unhealthy. The demands placed on the sales force were unrealistic. Competition among the sales staff was fierce and disloyalty was rampant. I quickly found out that most of the women working there stayed because they were highly paid, not because they enjoyed their work. Some had no choice, but I did.

I remember once helping a very wealthy couple. The manager showed up and insisted on showing them things they were not interested in looking at. Apparently an envious sales person in back had told the manager I did not know what I was doing and that these people could spend much more than what I was working on. This was not true. My gentler, easy-going attitude had won their trust and we had a good rapport.

In the case of shoppers like this, the policy was to make sure they were squeezed out of every dollar they could spend and the manager now wanted to make sure the policy was implemented. The sale amounted to $10,000 and I anticipated a large commission. But the following day I found a note on my locker telling me that I would only receive part of my commission because the manager had *had* to help me. Outraged, I quit the same day.

But I had learned about Sarasota's wealthy clientele. I understood their likes and dislikes, who was part of the Sarasota elite and who would become a friend. What I also learned from that experience was something about myself, that I had a hard time being surrounded by negative people. It strengthened my belief that I should strive as much as possible to have positive people around me. I felt that during the few months I worked in that shop, I aged a lot and the quality of my life was too important to ever take a job like that again.

While the politics at my job were still developing, I had to deal with where I would live. After work one evening, I found a notice on my door from the management of the complex asking all the tenants to attend a meeting that night. When I entered the club room I noticed a police officer standing in a corner. I sat with the other tenants and listened to the manager and a police inspector recall the gory details of a brutal rape which had happened four days before, in a building next to mine. It apparently was the second time an attack had happened in three weeks and the management of the complex was very concerned for the tenants. I had a hard time accepting the idea that these crimes had occurred less than two months after moving into the complex. I had chosen this part of town thinking it was safe and desirable as living alone, safety had always been a priority.

I was so upset that I decided I would be better off moving again and sped up the process of buying a house. I spent every Sunday looking at houses till I found a charming two bedroom house with a swimming pool and lots of potential. It took me fifteen minutes to make up my mind and I bought the house the same day. I moved in the week before Christmas and Robin promised he would join me on Christmas Eve.

The packing and unpacking turned out to be a challenge as I was still working all day and never had any time to get settled from my previous move three months before. But when Robin arrived on a windy night, my joy was complete.

As he got married late in life, he was usually able to spend Christmastime with me. This was a special time we shared together and I treasured the memories. Robin was a pleasure to have around. He kept a very youthful attitude and was always ready to do something new. I also felt so secure with him. His tall and sportive look generated respect from everybody around and, with his protective attitude, it was like having a bodyguard around. Later, when he got married, I was happy that life had given him a wonderful family, but I missed my bodyguard.

After I settled down, I also realized how wonderful it was to feel secure and safe, not afraid of break-ins at night. The family neighborhood I chose for my new home was quiet, far away from the downtown area and it gave the impression nothing ever happened there.

After I left my job on St. Armand circle, the move turned out to be another blessing. It had demanded organization on my part, but once that was out of the way, I was able to give all my attention to what I would do next. I wondered if opening another shop would be right for me. In fact, opening another business would be, by far, the best solution in the long run.

I gave myself a few months to do nothing but think and work on my new house. I always enjoyed remodeling and this was one time I did not want to rush. This time of rest also made me realize I would never be happy working for somebody else. I knew how to open new businesses and by this time I felt I had enough knowledge about it that I could not lose. I knew with certainty that this would be the best business I ever had.

The answer to my question was obvious long before I acknowledged it. So, at an age when some people start thinking of retirement, I started another *Belle de Jour* and it would be more rewarding than I ever thought.

I combed the town, area by area, street by street, walking and talking to people about locations with reasonable rents. Then one day, on a side street in the historic district, I stared at a corner space with a "For Rent" sign in the window. I could not believe how lucky I was because the area was becoming *the* place to be. One of the location's biggest assets, in addition to being at the corner of two busy streets, was that it had four huge display windows.

I signed the lease with an owner who kept asking if I knew what I was doing, as she thought it would not be a good place for fashion. She said my business would be a first for the area, which was home to antique dealers and decorators. I told her this was exactly what I wanted and it was an ideal place for what I had in mind.

When I took possession of my new shop I felt like an adventurer exploring a new land. But what people did not know was that I had a strong feeling of being right and that this piece of real estate was just what I needed. That feeling was difficult to explain, but whenever it occurred, I never failed. It was during times like this that I felt the force of the universe showing me the way. It was intoxicating to feel so sure. It also was the time I did my best, flying from one project to another with ease and eagerness.

As it turned out, I built a business that did, indeed, take off in a flash and ended up being extremely successful. Eight years later I sold it and retired much more comfortably because of it.

Chapter Twenty-Seven

Sunny Land of Florida

I t was close to the new millennium and two years had passed since I moved down to Sarasota. I started to feel as though I belonged there.

Philip and his family came every spring to spend a vacation with me and to enjoy the beautiful sands of Siesta Key beach. This was the highlight of my life, as I always had a great time with them. I would take off a few days from work and go to the beach to enjoy my grandson, Evan, splashing in the sea or building sand castles. As a grandmother, I fully enjoyed the privilege of spoiling him without the hassles of parenthood. Evan was a beautiful child and, as I watched him running on the beach, I could not help reflecting on my own children whom I had enjoyed so much. The emptiness left by their absence was never fulfilled. As life presented other joys, I adapted well. But like many other parents, I often looked at photo albums of my children in their new environments and new lives with a nostalgic feeling of years gone by.

Meanwhile, I was building my business and doing better than anticipated. I managed to pay off the bank loan after one year, put myself on a salary and was generous to my part-time employee. The business saw a twenty percent growth in profit every year and my reputation was also growing fast.

My success was not a coincidence but rather the result of a little ruse I played. As I was targeting a privileged clientele, I always made sure I carried one-of-a-kind, hand-painted items, hand-loomed sweaters and unusual clothing or jewelry designed by young designers whose prices were reasonable. While displaying the expensive things in the windows, I would stock the shop with much more affordable clothing. My theory was that by attracting the curious, I would end up selling the less expensive items. It worked well. Of course, I always had people who could afford the more luxurious items. But for the people who could not, they still felt great buying in an exclusive shop.

With my Dior training, I carried classic designs and not faddish items. Customers were treated like friends and often came in just to chat. A magazine wrote an article on the shop and on my background. It brought a lot of people in, including some of the best-known people in town.

Over the years I developed many friendships and loved running the business, which by now had two employees, a model showing my clothes in one of the best restaurants and part-time people helping now and then. My business was my life. I enjoyed it so much that I did not mind going back home exhausted at the end of the day, because I was pleased to feel needed and respected. I sometimes felt like a celebrity and basked in the warmth of well-meaning people.

In the summer, I closed the shop for two months and went traveling to Europe, or to some special place I felt like visiting. Once it was Alaska, another time I spent some time on a 100-year-old schooner called *The French*, while sailing the shores of Maine. Sometimes I would drive to Boston, Maine or New Hampshire, keeping in touch with old friends and stopping along the way to explore places I did not know.

This was the time I could enjoy my other grandchildren, Meaghan and Lexi. Robin and his wife Kim had moved from Connecticut to Florida, just an hour away from me, shortly after Meaghan was born. This baby had the most brilliant red hair I had ever seen and a smile that never ceased. She was a happy baby and used to love the audience and compliments she received when Kim stopped by the shop to show her off. Very early on, little Meaghan seemed to enjoy the attention her beautiful red hair created. It was such a treat to have Robin, Kim and Meaghan around.

Alexa-Nicole, or Lexi as we called her, was born in Florida. I will never forget the five o'clock morning phone call telling me they were at the hospital and wanted me to come right away. I was very excited as it was the first time I would see one of my grandchildren immediately after birth. While Kim and Robin were in the delivery room, I waited in Kim's room and was taken by surprise when a nurse came rushing in carrying Lexi, telling me she had to clean her up. The incredible joy I felt while watching the whole process was overwhelming. I had tears streaming down my cheeks when the nurse asked, "Would you like to hold her?" At that moment my world became complete.

As I was getting older, running the shop was becoming more difficult. The places I had to go ranged from Miami to New York, Atlanta to Dallas and a few smaller places. But the trips were becoming tiring and I wondered how long I could keep doing so much traveling. I had to start thinking of my retirement and get used to the idea that I would be alone, without a partner to keep me company, or a business to run. I was looking at Florida with new eyes, wondering what I was going to do there for the long run.

Knowing that businesses take a long time to sell, I thought I should list it with a broker and see what happened, hoping deep down it would not sell for a long time. Emotionally, I was not ready to retire. One has mixed emotions about these things. It was my whole career, my whole life and I enjoyed the business so much.

I did not know whether to go back to France or stay in the U.S., where my family was. Most of the French friends I met here were going back to their native country. It is hard to explain why people when they get older have such a desire to go back to their roots. Maybe it is a natural thing. I always had a great attraction to the south of France and could not stop thinking about it, until I realized how difficult it would be to leave my family behind. Travel was becoming difficult and turning out to be a luxury and I did not want the Atlantic Ocean to come between me and my family here in the U.S. So I put the whole idea of retiring in France out of my head and concentrated on my business, with its traveling and all.

Chapter Twenty-Eight

The End of a Career

On a beautiful February morning I went to work early. Catching up on paperwork and other routine activities was my goal for the next two hours. But as I approached the door to the shop, I heard the phone ring. Who could be calling at 8:30 in the morning? My customers were not the early type and would not call before eleven in the morning. I was curious to know who was prompting me to accelerate my pace to answer the phone.

A voice I did not recognize made sure I was the owner of *Belle de Jour* before telling me to wait for her boss to come to the phone. When he introduced himself, I recognized the name of the broker who listed my business sale three months earlier. After this much time, I had assumed my business was too small to be of interest to him and deep down I was happy about it, since I was sad to let it go. But he said he had an excellent buyer whom he wanted to bring in to look at the shop. The buyer also wanted to meet with me the following morning.

The phone call made me conscious of the fact that I had signed a contract and was obligated to show the business to a prospective buyer. My first thought was that this would not necessarily end up in a sale, so I tried not to worry. But on the other hand it could and the idea of not having my business any more brought tears to my eyes.

The next morning I hurried to be on time to meet the potential buyer. Two people were waiting at the front door, five minutes early. I recognized my broker but was surprised to see a young woman in her thirties with him. The nature of my business attracted an older clientele, so I expected to meet a more mature buyer. After introductions, the broker left us to talk for about two hours. Her candid questions prompted me to face reality, but did not prepare me for what happened next.

Four hours later, I received a phone call that an offer was on the way and would be presented to me that night. Surprise was not what I felt. Shocked beyond belief would be a better description. I sat down, wiped away a few tears and prepared myself to face the consequences of what I had started months before.

The broker arrived and told me he had never seen an offer come so hastily regarding the acquisition of a business. I read the contract and another surprise awaited me. She wanted to close in ten days, with no contingencies. My offer to stay with the business for thirty days was reduced to fifteen and the all-cash offer was very close to my asking price. There was no reason for me not to accept such an impressive offer. I had twenty four hours to return the contract signed and I knew I would never get another one like this. So I signed and joined the ranks of so many Floridians, becoming a retiree.

For two weeks I tried to share the secrets of my success with the new owner. But she was not interested. I got the feeling she thought she knew everything and wanted to change the entire concept of the business. It was hers, after all, but I just kept hoping she knew what she was doing.

Now I was left to wonder, what was I going to do without the pleasure and the joy of my life achievement? Those first few weeks brought panic into my life. How could I, all of a sudden, stop doing what I loved so much? How could I survive without a steady income? The proceeds of the sale of the business brought me some immediate security but would not be enough to keep me in the lifestyle I was accustomed to for very long. I started to have nightmares and for the first time I felt fear for my future. I forgot the universe always took care of me.

Endless Beginnings

Feeling sorry for myself was not a familiar element in my life. Meditating helped me regain peace of mind. After two weeks of distress, I concentrated on the miracle that had just happened. The sale of my business was a perfect ending to an adventure that had taken me further than I expected and along the way had given me the satisfaction of knowing I made a difference in the lives of many people. All the years of working so hard had given me the respect of my suppliers, as well as the reputation of keeping my word. It gave me a sense of contentment and I began to reminisce about the many blessings I gained from a rich and rewarding career.

Among the stories I like to recall, one in particular comes to mind that I will never forget. It happened in Boston in the seventies. One of my younger customers was getting married and on one occasion when she came to the shop, she told me her mother had become very sick and she needed my help. The wedding had been changed and would take place shortly at the hospital, where her mother was in a wheelchair, in a critical state.

She wanted me to choose a dress for her mother for the occasion. I had never met the woman and there was little time left. After asking her some questions, I decided on a dress I knew could be refitted for someone in a wheel-chair and happened to be made in her mother's favorite blue color. It was a difficult task to dress someone I did not know, but I was determined to make it work, as I could see the anxiety on my client's face. Once again, I followed my instincts.

Two weeks after delivering the dress and I had nearly forgotten about it, my young customer walked in and put her arms around me and said, "Thank you," over and over again. She explained that the wedding had taken place a week before. When her mother saw the dress, her face lit up and she smiled. She said she had not seen her mother like this in months. The joy of seeing her mother happy and smiling again was overwhelming and she came to share her joy with me. Fighting her tears back, she said her mother died the day after the wedding.

Then there were the glamorous people I met, such as the dress designer for the movie *The Great Brinks Robbery* in Boston in 1976. She did not have a dress for herself for the premiere of the movie, which happened to be that very night. She bought one of my own designs to wear and it made me proud to hear her tell me how much she loved it.

Another time, in Florida, Stephen King came in looking for a present for his wife on her birthday and he made everybody in the shop laugh with his great sense of humor. I had not recognized him at first and asked him to please wait his turn. I suppose my behavior might have lacked some of the admiration he usually generated. But when he handed me his American Express card with his name on it, I realized who he was and could only smile to apologize for my rudeness. He flashed a big smile and simply said, "No problem at all."

How could I ever forget so many faces along the road of a thirty-year career? On and off they were the ones I spent my time with, from the opening of my first shop to the closing of the last one. I felt fortunate to have been given the privilege to work with so many wonderful women.

Three of them are still very close friends. Terry, Jean and Mary Ann still call regularly. Yet I miss working with them. No one was more blessed than I for having such amazing people working for me. Those women were gifts, sent to me when I needed them the most.

The universe offered lessons that were hard for me to learn. But when I finally got its messages, I was paid back many times over. Diamonds could have never been as precious as knowing I was never alone and was always guided along the way.

I know there was a purpose to what I did. I helped lots of women become surer of themselves. By coaching them, teaching them some simple rules of fashion and helping them choose the right look, they felt and carried themselves better. Their pleasure was my reward. I was privileged that they learned to trust me.

I believe everybody in life has a special purpose, a special talent or gift to share with others. For many years I could not see what my purpose was. It was only much later that I understood that what we accomplish in life does not have to be extraordinary. Just following our heart, our instincts and doing the right thing, eventually draws a path leading us to what we are good at. The satisfaction I received from following these principles far exceeded the pains I felt for so many years, asking myself what I was here for.

As for the business that was now in the hands of another, it did not do well after I sold it. It has since then been resold again, hopefully for the best. I still feel attached to the memory and would love to know the venture I put my heart and soul into for so many years will continue to grow for a long time to come.

Sarasota, Florida. My last store

In Florida in my sixties

Part Five

Chapter Twenty-Nine

What Next?

For many years now, I have learned to live alone, but it was a choice. I felt for a long time that I had not learned how to love someone else enough, to get the right partner in my life. I had known several long-term relationships, but for some reasons, I always had the feeling that I was not ready to give what was needed to another to make a final commitment. I saw women sacrificing their lives for their sick older husbands and I always felt I would have a hard time doing that. Being alone and independent gave me the opportunity to explore and experiment with situations that I might not have been able to do in a relationship; unless I would have found someone who would have truly understood my independence. At times it is a hard price to pay, as loneliness becomes more real as we age.

There were never-ending beginnings in my relationships just like in my professional life and where I lived. Why did I always have to push the envelope and strive for more? Was I born with an insatiable desire to explore and not settle for what I already had?

I wonder sometimes if there was more I could have done. Might there have been other lessons to be learned? Did I always get the right signals? Where do we draw the line between selfishness and self-fulfillment?

I believe my destiny and the wellbeing of my soul were very much tied together. I had to constantly ask questions and not take anything for granted. I do not believe I achieved a sense of clarity by chance. I had to experience pains and solitude in order to get where I am today.

Home is a nostalgic word for me. Looking back into my past, there were very few times I felt totally at home. Torn apart between two worlds, I only felt at home when I was raising my family. I could let go of France and my European family then. My children were my home.

But after my divorce and a life so full of moves, I could not associate the word 'home' with any place in particular. I replaced the word with a feeling of being happy and comfortable wherever I lived. Home is a state of mind. It is when a warm feeling of wellbeing invades me, when I know my children are happy, when the sun shines through my windows, when a little child smiles at me and when peace surrounds me. Home is inside of me and I can transport it anywhere. Wherever I live, when I am happy I am home and it allows me to appreciate my blessings.

I have been blessed with the most wonderful children and grandchildren one could wish for. This was not luck. This was my reward because what I did for my children was agonizing, separating myself from them for so many years. But I did the right thing. I was not a great mother. But I tried to be the best I could for the family. After my divorce I would have loved to go back to France, but I stayed because I loved my children so much. They had a good father whom they needed as much as they needed me. While they were growing up, I often asked the universe to take care of them, knowing in the end that they would be wonderful human beings. My faith and belief were so strong that it could not have been any other way.

I also received other rewards in my career and in my friendships. I was blessed with the best. So facing retirement late in life was not any more stressful.

—⁂—

Florida had been my home for ten years and I faced another beginning. After working very hard for thirty-five years, it was difficult to get my mind and my imagination to slow down. I needed much more than what Florida could offer me. I wanted to pursue my education, learn more about life itself and start writing. Florida did not feel like the right place to pursue my new goals. What should I do next? The universe was silent and my imagination was not helping me. But I knew eventually I would be guided.

With mixed feelings, I considered going back to France because life is easier for older people there. For two months, I searched the internet for a house to buy in the south of France. While planning my new project I kept avoiding the thought of leaving my children and grandchildren behind, thinking I could go back to the States often, but I was having a hard time accepting the fact that I would not see them as often as I wanted to.

The universe had other plans for me and in a powerful way changed the course of my life. The first sign was economic. The dollar fell to an all-time low while French properties went up to an all-time high. The combination of both made it impossible to go on with my plan. So I had to explore new avenues.

I searched the internet for someplace else in the U.S. It would need to have stimulating things for me to do to replace my involvement in my business. Going back up to New England was not a possibility because of the harsh weather. Plus, my best friends, had left Boston to go back to France. So it would have to be a new place.

Some strong forces were at work when I attended a dinner party one night. A couple talked about moving to "The Triangle" and I did not know what they were talking about. When they mentioned Duke University and Chapel Hill, I started to pay attention. They had gone there several times and were looking for a house to buy. I asked them many questions and listened with great interest to their reasons for wanting to move there.

They had found the people in North Carolina to be gentle, caring and generally happy to live there. The resources for culture and education were endless. A bulb turned on in my head. This conversation made me realize I wanted a university town. It helped me decide what to do in the next few months and where I was going to live. The following week, I was on my way to North Carolina to start exploring.

My guiding star had given me direction and now it was up to me to do the rest. In this case, I had the help of more "coincidences," starting with finding a real estate agent who spoke French fluently and really knew what I wanted. In two months I found the right house in Durham. At the same time, my Florida house sold near the asking price, despite the rough real estate market. Pieces were falling into place magically, so it was time to say goodbye to many friends. The severing of cherished ties was difficult.

But Florida had not always been easy. Despite all the people I interacted with, I often felt alone. I had led a busy life, not really wanting to get involved and I kept my distance. I accepted invitations to go to parties, but did not spend enough time with my friends. I built walls around me. I think it was often part of a hectic contemporary life style. Like other people in business who stop working, they find that when the walls come down, reality sets in. These walls were meant to protect me, but instead, they isolated me and were responsible for my loneliness.

I moved in October and everything went without a glitch. Durham was called *The City of Medicine*, Raleigh had all the best museums and trappings of a big city and Chapel Hill had the charm of a southern city mixed with the flavor of foreign and domestic students. Then, of course, the Research Triangle had all the latest high-tech businesses, attracting people from all over the world. What a pleasure it was for me to become part of this ambiance.

As soon as I arrived I was lucky enough to find people who guided me towards Duke University and all the events offered. They had courses for adult education, foreign movies, single groups and had a lot of great resources. There were also many interesting people who had traveled all over the world and my being French was not so foreign to them. In a short time I made friends and felt there was so much to do I would not have time to miss my old career.

As I reflect on my life and what brought me there, I saw a

quiet place, one that helped me to better understand the contrast of joys and hardships in my life, like yin and yang. My new heaven helped me write, read and enjoy life fully.

But three years after I moved to Durham, life had another move for me, this time caused by my younger son's health. We never know when an extra lesson might come; we just have to accept that it always is for the best.

On a winter day in Hartford, Connecticut, Robin had a stroke. He was forty-five and seemed to be in perfect health. I drove back and forth to Hartford until I finally realized that I needed to remain nearby. So I made the decision to leave a city I adored and prepared once more to find a place to live closer to my children. Thanks to the right treatment, today Robin is doing very well. I would have loved to stay in North Carolina, but at the time there was no choice. I could not be so far from my son.

I finally settled in Cape Cod. It was only three hours from Hartford and the weather was not as harsh as Boston's. I needed a place where I could retire in a quiet environment and Connecticut never appealed to me.

Cape Cod was the right choice. It was a haven for retirees and had much to offer through its symphony, a very good college and an active artist's community. The cold, snow and ice would not be enough to make me dislike my new home. I found new friends and most of all, a place close to my children and grandchildren, who come often to visit. So, once more, joy filled my heart.

Joy can come in small doses, or sometimes, as in this case, it invades so fully that your heart feels like it is going to explode. I always feel grateful when this feeling of wellbeing invades me and I know it is a reward for hard work.

Chapter Thirty

Climbing the Lembert Dome

Before I get to the end of this book, I want to talk about great joys.

In 1989, before being transferred by his firm to California, my son Philip called to tell me he had a few days before starting his work and he was planning to go to Yosemite to climb the Lembert Dome. He was twenty-eight then and wanted to know if I was in sufficiently good shape to go with him. My first reaction was to answer that my sedentary lifestyle had not prepared me for outdoor sports. But when he added, "Dad could never do it, he's so out of shape, but I thought you might want to give it a try," my ears prickled. Andrew and I had been divorced for nine years but still were not talking to each other at that time. The idea that my son thought I could do something his father could not was a temptation.

Without hesitation I said, "Of course I can do it." My heart was pounding when I answered, as I knew this adventure could turn out to be very difficult. I had three weeks to prepare for an adventure that was totally out of character for me.

The first thing I did was to buy the best pair of sneakers I could find. In my world of fashion and real estate, I had never owned a pair and proudly decided this was to be a turning point. Then I woke up early every morning and followed one of the physical regimens offered on television by the latest sports guru of the time. This was hard. I had not exercised in years and I found myself waking up in the morning feeling my whole body crying, "Stop, stop, you're killing me." But I was determined to get myself into shape. After one week, I started to feel better and had made enough progress to realize it was only a matter of time before I could bend, run, jump and follow the leader without huffing and puffing. By the time Philip arrived I had totally improved my physical condition and felt I was fit to go with him.

We left early on a Saturday morning and the excitement of going on an adventure with my son was one of the greatest thrills I had had in a long time. Philip was very close to his dad and at times I felt estranged from my older son. I thought this trip taken together could be the best thing for our relationship.

We decided to go directly to the Lembert Dome first, climb it and then look at the rest of the park afterward. We knew it would take about four to five hours to get back from the climb. So we reserved rooms in a nearby motel and planned to go back to the park the following morning to explore what we missed the first day.

After parking the car, we prepared for our climb. The bottom of the mountain had a small grassy path leading to another path that became steeper as we walked. It seemed to me that the steep patch of grass we started from would never end. But as we kept climbing, it was evident that this last part of the climb was leading to the stone dome on the mountain high above us. Gallantly, Philip from time to time would ask me if I needed a rest along the way, but I always refused as I knew I would need to stop further up the mountain.

When we finally reached the area of the hike on solid granite, our pace changed radically. The lower part was a matter of climbing over earth and smaller rocks, one on top of the other. But as we came closer to the top, it became much more difficult. Using feet, knees, hands and arms, I pulled myself to the large dome-like area that gave the mountain its name. When I arrived there, I realized there was only one way for me to climb it and that was by crawling like a crab on all fours.

There were four or five people at the top, looking down at us.

They were young and laughing. I suppose they were laughing at me for the awkward way I was pulling myself to the top. When they realized I was a mature fifty-something-year-old lady, I heard one of them offering his help. Slightly put out by the offer, I answered I was doing well and did not need assistance.

I did make it to the top and the incredible joy of having done something different, slightly dangerous, but so exciting, was overwhelming. As I was catching my breath I looked around and never in my life had I seen such beauty. The combination of this exciting climb, the beauty of the mountains, the clear blue sky, the joy of having my son to share this experience with and the pure fresh air all made for a day I would never forget.

I felt on top of the world. At that moment everything was suspended in time and I got the feeling I could touch the stars or a few angels who had lost their way, curiously flying towards the earth. If I could describe pure joy, this was it for me; the joy of being totally part of something greater, when the senses all join together to create a feeling of wellbeing and ecstasy.

It is during moments of happiness such as this one that I best understand the power of the elements surrounding us, the power of the earth and of the entire universe. This is when my heart is so full of gratitude that I feel like shouting, "Thank you, thank you." I can easily forget the pains and troubles I have been through in my life, but never the great joys.

The following day, we spent the entire day exploring the beauty and the marvel of Yosemite's rocks and trees. The stone granite walls looked like they had been cut by chain saws. The crystal clear rivers and the grassy paths undulating around them created scenarios which would have brought joy and inspiration to the greatest painters.

We finally had to go back, as Philip was going to start his job after the weekend. When we did, I left knowing that this incredible weekend would lighten up my life for a long time. Nature brought a new dimension. Earthquakes and hurricanes taught me to respect the fury of the elements, but being at the top of a mountain taught me something else about the incredible beauty of the world we live in. Beauty is like peace. It gives feelings of wellbeing, of being complete, of being closer to the true meaning of life.

Today when I look at the pictures of the trip remembering how wonderful it was, I see similarities between climbing to the top of the mountain and the search to better understand our destiny. The hardships, the excitement and the rewards are the same.

Crawling like a crab up Lembert Dome

Near the top

Chapter Thirty-One

Peace

I n September 2008, I went back to France for a visit. As the
plane landed in Paris at Charles de Gaulle airport, I noticed a
change in how I felt about returning to my native country. The
excitement I'd felt in my previous visits was replaced by a quiet
sense of happiness, not the excitement of going *home*. Maybe
a long sleepless night was the reason for this change. But that
reason did not seem right. It was something different. *I* had
changed.

I realized that my heart had become American and I looked
at things differently. I was no longer torn apart between two
worlds as I now knew where I belonged. It did not take me long
to realize this was my new perspective.

I could not wait to see if this trip was going to teach me more
about what I had become and if it also would be a reflection of
the inner peace I felt. In the past, the time I spent in France had
brought me both joy and pain. I wondered if I would now be
able to enjoy just the positive experiences, the ones I treasured
most. I was hoping it would.

Before going to Paris to see my family, I visited with some
friends. When my plane landed in Nice with a thump and a
squeal of rubber, I felt excited at the idea of seeing Yannick and
Dominique, who were waiting for me at the airport to take me
to their home in Antibes. I had known Yannick since we were
both fifteen, long enough that she felt like part of my family. Her

favorite distraction, bridge, was a gift in which she had really excelled. I introduced her to her husband, Dominique. He was an earthy type and I never heard him say anything bad about anybody in his life. These dear friends were always a pleasure to visit and laugh with. Their home was built in the 1800s on lots of acreage before it was divided. It was one of the first homes in Antibes.

Their daughter Nathalie, an artist and my god child, lived nearby. I had the chance to visit her and spend some time admiring her latest sculptures.

I left them to visit another great friend, Nicole (I have a few friends named Nicole), who lives only a few miles away from them. She and her husband, however, are one of the couples who had moved from Boston back to France. They now spend a few months a year in their home in Scituate, Massachusetts, to keep up with their American heritage.

Nicole and Radu's children live all over the world and are prominent figures in Eastern Europe. Over the years the family has done a lot for Romania, where Radu is from and is highly respected. Radu is a well-known writer who has written many books about Romania and the legend of Dracula.

Radu was away when I went to visit Nicole, so it was just the two of us for a few days. She took me around and during one of our tours, showed me an incredible house, built by one of the Rothschilds at the turn of the century. This small palace was built on a hill overlooking the Mediterranean, in Villefranche-sur-Mer. A long basin filled with water, reminiscent of the Taj Mahal, draws the eyes to the front of the house. Ten different gardens surround this paradise. I had never heard of this jewel before and was glad Nicole took me there to visit. We spent a delightful time walking through the exotic Japanese garden and a few other gardens, each one representing a different part of the world. The beauty of the scenery and the deep blue Mediterranean were breathtaking. At the end of the afternoon, we went back to my friends' villa, in Antibes, where I took a dip in the pool to end a perfect day.

After visiting with my friends, I went to see my family. I

left Antibes on the high speed train, which only took five hours to Paris. The speed reached over 150 miles per hour at times, but the ride was smooth and uneventful. My brother Roby was waiting for me at the station and we drove to his home where I would be spending the next few days. He was in the best of moods and I rejoiced in spending a few moments alone with him.

Roby was not always easy to be with, but on that day he had his sense of humor and this reminded me of some of the better times we had together, when we were younger. We had dinner with most of the gang, which included his wife, Marielle and their children Eulalie and Charles. Their older son, Gabriel, was absent as he was spending his holidays in Corsica.

From there, I went to visit my sister. I knew this would be difficult, as she had been battling cancer for several years and was getting worse. I felt her pain and listened to the stories she shared with me. There was not much I could say to make the situation better for her. I went to visit her at the nursing home for four days in a row, keeping in mind the situation was not only sad but desperate. Because her eyes did not work properly, she spent hours staring at the ceiling without being able to do anything. Her physical pain was taken care of with morphine patches worn around the clock. Bringing her gifts and flowers brought a smile to her face, but this was the only time I saw her smile.

My sister and I have held different beliefs and it was difficult to find words to ease her anguish. But during this visit I could accept our differences. It was not up to me, nor the right time, to share with her my philosophy. As I said good bye, I took away with me the image of a tortured human being I love but could not help.

Every year or two, I go back to see my sister and I always leave with the awareness that it might be the last time. It brings the same familiar emotions as before, when my mother died. Once more in my life I am faced with the fact that cancer is taking away someone I love, in a country far away from where I live. I feel powerless as there is nothing I can do.

As I was going through my emotions during that visit, I became aware that I was unusually calm, sad but composed, but above all, at peace with what was going on around me. The turmoil affecting my family stirred my compassion, but deep down, I knew there was nothing I could do but listen to them.

My brother and his wife lived just a few miles away from our sister, so they have been with her constantly and have lived the trauma for a long time. I felt bad for them as well as for my sister.

A few more friends came to visit me while I was in Paris and I was thankful to have such faithful friends. These friendships were gifts to me.

Preparing to leave, I was filled with gratitude. As difficult as it had been to see my sister in such despair, I could not help but notice a real change in the attitude my family had towards me. I felt loved.

Previous trips had always been difficult, as both my brother and sister made me feel inadequate. They never asked for my advice, nor were they much interested in what I was doing in the States. They often treated me like a stranger. At least it was the impression I got in the past.

This time it felt different. There was interest in what I was doing and my brother treated me like he was proud of me. After years of misunderstandings, I felt accepted and respected. Did they change?

Or did I change? In the past I might have expected too much. Or they might have thought that my lifestyle was different from theirs. I had to keep in mind that I was the one who went away. How could I have expected them to see life through my eyes?

As we age, values change. At this point in my life, I find that many of the emotions we share are the same.

For so long I had searched for love and peace. Towards the end of my life I accomplished both. I felt the universe offered me a tough bargain, but in the end the gifts I received far exceeded the difficulties. So, I flew back home with a great sense of peace and happiness for all the joys and serenity I received, keeping a positive attitude about all the experiences I went through during my trip.

Chapter Thirty-Two

Putting It Together

The story of my life has been about new beginnings and each new beginning has been about lessons learned along the way. They have often been painful but in the end they served their purpose and left me with a sense of gratitude, fulfillment and peace.

As a child I was spiritually programmed by my parents, who took me to church. Everything would have been simple if I could have just followed the family traditions, stayed with my own people and culture and not searched for answers to my many questions.

The fantasy life I had built while growing up contributed to my restlessness as an adult. There was so much to see and learn and I yearned for an extraordinary life. It was not so much for glory. But without understanding exactly why, I felt I had a lot to share. Maybe the fact that nobody listened to me when I was growing up built a reservoir of untold stories.

To me, life was confusing. There were too many people with different thoughts, philosophies and religions. I realized early in life we were not in control of our destiny. When I was six, my parents and I were on our way to visit my grandmother and, while crossing the street, I let go of their hands and dashed ahead of them. A car hit me and I fell. During the confusion that followed, I remember thinking how lucky I was to be unharmed and safe. This feeling of being lucky stayed with me for the rest of my life and perhaps was the catapult that gave me the courage to explore and live differently from the rest of my family.

Luck is not about having all your desires met. Rather, it is about going through difficulties and knowing you will come out on top. Luck is given to us by the universe. It is a gift.

My mother used to say that I was like a cat, falling upright all the time, or getting back on my feet right away. In a way she was right. No matter how difficult a situation I found myself in, I never gave up and I always believed in finding a solution to every problem that presented itself. What was an automatic response as a child became more rational as the years passed.

Thirty years later, when I took the Silva method course at the age of thirty seven, it all came together in my mind. I found out that I was in total control of my life. I created all of the situations and events in my life. I could never blame somebody else for my failures. But I also knew how proud I should be of my success. There would be no way of appreciating success, happiness or joy without knowing the hardship of failures, mistakes and sorrows.

New beginnings often happen following changes in our lives and are sometimes difficult to manage. Other times we make the choice to improve our present situation. In both cases new decisions have to be made in order to survive.

Stagnancy could be the fate of those who avoid the challenges of life and do not see better horizons ahead. I know quite a few people who are satisfied in the knowledge that every day of their lives is exactly the same. They are happy avoiding new perspectives and I sometimes envy their attitude. Changes are scary and demand courage and determination, as well as an adventurous mind and openness to new ideas and thoughts. We know what we have but can only guess the outcome of a new situation when we dare to step into the unknown.

The choices we make draw new maps into our lives and we can rarely return to our old way of thinking. The life we knew before making changes took its own path. It is no longer what we want.

The more I learned my way and gained confidence in my

judgment, the stronger I felt about the success of a new enterprise and the better the outcome. It was only when I had doubts, felt unsure or needed a new lesson that difficulties appeared in my life.

The most difficult decision I ever made was to move to California, because it meant living far away from my children. My divorce was final and after a short time Andrew had more control over my sons than was acceptable to me. It also seemed he was influencing them too much. It was a bad arrangement and I did not know what to do. There was no doubt in my mind that something had to be done. I believe the dramatic choice of moving three thousand miles away was critical for the peace of mind and mental health of both my sons and I. Only the certainty that it was the best thing to do at the time helped me make my decision. I also felt pushed and guided gently. I am sure it was not the only path I could have taken, but at the time it felt like the only one. I am glad things improved later for the better, but I believe they could have become worse if I did not have the courage to leave.

There were harsh consequences to pay. The price was that, on and off, I missed eight years of their presence, with the exception of vacations. It also interfered with our relationships and took years to repair the damage. Until finally, one after the other, at two different times, my sons moved in with me in California.

Today andrew and I are friends and often talk about the joys we share, our children and grandchildren. Everyone in the family feels loved and supported. The hurt of the past is long forgotten. Andrew and I were teachers to each other and I can only hope he learned from me as much as I learned from him. I will always be grateful to him.

There were times in my life when I thought I did everything right and still suffered. In 2007, for the second time, I was diagnosed with breast cancer. I ate nutritious food, exercised, meditated, tried to better myself and was quite confident I could keep illness away. But I had to be tested again. I still had to learn more. The words of Gregg Tiffin heard thirty before, were still etched in my mind: "....but you will be given the strength and the power you will need." Was this what I was supposed to learn? Where did I ever get the idea that following the rules would spare me pain?

I had to walk through doubts, traumas and joys to finally know that spiritual laws were sometimes confusing but always worked. I could never ignore the fact that I had been saved from death several times in my life. I remembered an airplane crash I had a reservation on, flying back from Philadelphia to New York in 1959. I had forgotten to reconfirm my seat, so it was given to somebody else. The plane crashed with no survivors. And, of course, there was that terrible attack by armed men in California and the botched operation after which I was saved by an experimental drug.

As I reflect on these beginnings, I know that the lessons learned were instrumental in changing my character. By listening to my inner voice I always knew when I stepped out of line or missed my mark, giving me a chance to make things right. By meditating I chose to have the universe guide me. By not following a standard religion I gave myself a chance to understand the wisdom of many religions. It gave me a chance to explore more avenues that are still foreign to a lot of people. I learned about the laws of attraction that life is like a magnet sending us what we need to know and that we receive what we first send out into the world.

Over a lifetime I developed faith in myself, allowing me to better understand universal laws. It was by trusting my instincts that I learned to recognize the signs showing me the way. Now, as I enter the sunset of my life, it is not hard to accept the rules of the universe, as I know that they exist for the advancement of our souls. The "gold" I found along my journey was peace and for that I will forever be grateful.

Chapter Thirty-Three

My Universal Laws

These are the rules that work for me.

- Every day, take fifteen minutes to meditate.
- Always start by being thankful for all the people and wonderful things in your life. Then ask to be able to give more love and joy to others and learn how to receive more love and joy yourself. Then take a moment to concentrate on the people who need help. Finally, spend seventeen seconds visualizing what you truly care to have (the seventeen seconds rule was a suggestion I read in a book, as it is difficult to concentrate for that much time and reflect on how strongly your desire is.)
- Learn to love the people who hurt you. Visualize them on a stage in front of you, far away so that it makes it easier and send them thoughts of love. It becomes easier after a while.
- Remember to do to others those things you would want done to you.
- Believe that you can get everything you want. Have faith in the universe. It works for you, not against you.
- Doubt is antithetical to your power. This is a powerful

law. Having doubts about something stops the power that is given to you.

- When you don't get something, generally it is because there is a strong lesson to be learned from its lack.
- Visualization and details are the key to a successful journey.
- No matter what happens, never give up.
- Be patient.
- Desire is like a seed; it needs time to grow. This one was the hardest for me.
- Smile. Everywhere. At people you don't know, at home, alone or not.
- Practice being happy.
- Always be thankful. Even for the little things. The more you are, the more you get.
- Learn to recognize signs showing you the way. When you really believe in this, you can eventually learn to recognize genuine signs and not the product of your imagination.
- Believe in miracles. Coincidences are miracles sent your way. Always be thankful when they happen.
- Recognize that you are being guided and that help is always provided in the most difficult moments. You are never alone.
- Be generous. There is plenty in the universe. Even when you have little, you can always afford to give a compliment.
- Above all, have faith that you will always be taken care of.